Gunfire
and
Silence
Surviving India's 9/11

Douglas O'Keeffe

Cover artwork and title page by Arjen Eshuis

Edited by Alessandra Baglioni and Joanne Gaddy

First Printing, 2015

ISBN-13: 978-1514398487

CreateSpace, an Amazon company

ACKNOWLEDGEMENTS

Many people got me through the terrorist attack in Mumbai and its aftermath. I would like to thank:

My crew with whom I survived the attack, the crew that flew us out of Mumbai to Amsterdam, and the crew that flew us from Amsterdam to the United States.

My Leather family: Joanne Gaddy, Jose (Joee) Artega, Dean Ogren, and Don and Rob.

My brother Andy Lenart, my sister-in-law Urska Lenart, my mom and dad.

My flight attendant friends: Daryl, Lilly, Kari, Erik, and Jessica.

My Dutch friends: Ronald, Arjen, and Leo.

Alessandra Baglioni and Joanne Gaddy for their work on this book.

PREFACE

Gunfire and Silence, Surviving India's 9/11 is based upon actual events. I was in the Trident-Oberoi Hotel on November 26, 2008, when terrorists attacked it along with other locations in Mumbai. I'm a flight attendant for a major US airline, and I was in Mumbai on a layover. My crew and I arrived in Mumbai at midnight November 26 and were scheduled to leave the city 25 hours later at 1:00 am on November 27. The attack on the hotel and upon other locations occurred at about 10:00 pm, shortly before my crew members and I were scheduled for pick up to be driven to the airport for our departing flight.

The events I depict in this book are real and accurate as I recall them. I'm telling the story from my own perspective. My perspective does not reflect the official version of events nor the version of events experienced by other unfortunates caught in the attack. The names of the crew members and some other principles have been changed for privacy. Other characters were created for dramatic purposes. All the photos included are from my personal collection.

Please enjoy Gunfire and Silence, Surviving India's 9/11.

CAST OF CHARACTERS

My Crew:
Captain Daniel Abbott
First officer Sam Wilson
Second officer Ian Reid
Purser Nicolas Dumont
F/A Juan Lopez
F/A Tony Park
F/A Mary McAlister
F/A Colleen Ballard (her daughter Lisa who didn't go with us)
F/A Paula Burns
F/A David Johnson (his wife Shannon)
F/A Douglas O'Keeffe

Nigerian couple: Ladi and Fola Sheyabu
Ladi's mother, Miriam

Flight 36 crew:
Captain Marvin Ross
F/A Debra Welsh
F/A Samantha King, (her sister Teresa)
F/A Anne Fitzsimmons

Mumbai Airport station manager Raj Kansupada

German International Airlines Crew:
Purser Regina Schumann (husband Lutz)
Second purser Katrin Sammler, (ex-husband Fritz)
Junior F/A Nina Hoffman, (fiancé Joachim)
Other F/As: Barbara Weiler, Monika Klouse, Heike Muller, Christiane
Schmidt, Elisa Rau, Angelica Sebastian, Sandy Lutmann

F/A Heidi Low, Alpine International Air

Detroit personnel:
Detroit flight attendant base director Nancy Sullivan
Counter receptionist Shauna McNalley

Minneapolis personnel:
Richard Santini, director of airline security

Jim Snodgrass, assistant to Richard Santini
Margaret Olsen, director of disaster response team
Candice Price, receptionist to airline security office

My friends in Chicago:
Joanne Gaddy
Joee Arteaga
Don and Rob
Dean Ogren

Andrew Lenart, my brother in Missouri and Urska, his wife

Mina Sherafudin, counter agent in Taj Mahal Hotel and at current hotel

Sanjay Sheshadray, general manager Trident-Oberoi Hotel

Lynn Van Dermotten, my Dutch friend from training

Yvonne Ancey, my other friend from training

Amsterdam friends, Ronald, Leo and Arjen

My training roommates, Miguel and Bobby

Russel, my ex and former roommate

Orlando Sherman, my F/A friend in Detroit

Jessica Thompson, my F/A friend who saw me in the AMS hotel lobby

Douwe, and Alex, Netherlands International Airlines managers in AMS

Najeema, the crew accommodations woman at the Trident who dies in the attack

Amil, the leather shop proprietor in the Trident Oberoi Hotel
Mr. Gupta, proprietor of the jewelry shop in the Trident Oberoi Hotel

Paul Bjornmark from Sweden (his wife Eva), and Umesh Parwari businessman from Delhi, with whom Tony is stuck for two days

Prologue

Mumbai, formerly known as Bombay and the most populous city in India, was bustling on July 26, 2012, with its usual fervor of traffic, commerce, and people engaged in pleasurable pursuits. On that humid summer day, wearing blue jean shorts, a plain brown summer shirt, and flip-flop sandals, I felt underdressed in the elegant lobby of the Trident-Oberoi Hotel. I had made an appointment with the general manager, Sanjay Sheshadray, to visit the hotel, the site of a day I'll never forget. I knew I didn't have a lot of time that day. Being a flight attendant on a 24-hour airline layover, I'd arrived at midnight and was due to leave at 1:00 am the following morning. A fellow flight attendant, Laura Adams, sat with me in the lobby. When Mr. Sheshadray approached us, I stood to introduce myself. He greeted us, using the traditional Indian word "Namaste," pressing his fingertips together in the accompanying "praying hands" gesture. I failed to reciprocate instead extending my hand to him. As we awkwardly shook hands, I thanked him for meeting me and introduced Laura who, I explained, was with me for moral support as I faced the past. Graciously, he escorted us to the hotel's mezzanine level, exchanging small talk as we walked.

In the hall on the mezzanine level, he opened a door. "I think this is the room," he said. Glancing inside, I saw a large dining room with many tables and a small army of housekeepers swarming about dusting and sweeping. "No, I'm sorry, it's not," I responded. I was slightly disappointed, wondering whether he actually knew which room I wanted to see. "Ah, then it's over here!" he exclaimed, turning to a door a few steps across the wide hall. Using his key to unlock the door, he swung it open. As I looked into the room, my body froze and my eyes glazed over. I inhaled and said, "This is it. This is it." I wasn't seeing the empty room before me, though. I saw the room as it had been on November 26, 2008, when we were huddled there hoping the rescuers would arrive before the terrorists found us.

~ ~ ~

Flying had been my dream for many years; finally, the blue skies called to me. Before I was hired by Trans International Airlines, I was living in Cleveland and working as a legal assistant at a downtown Cleveland law firm. I had just turned 30, and my job wasn't going anywhere. I felt under-utilized. So in July 1996, the week after my birthday, I applied to four airlines. In short order, three of them rejected me (ironically, by 2009 one of the rejecting airlines merged with TIA, so I ended up working for an airline that had rejected me!). A week later, a representative from TIA called to invite me to a group interview in Minneapolis on Tuesday, August 20.

Being absent from the law firm would be a challenge, but I knew I had to try. I quickly negotiated an agreement with my boss to put in extra hours that week in order to complete my work and receive my full paycheck. TIA sent me a ticket, and I flew to Minneapolis. Upon arrival, I made my way to the arranged meeting point and surveyed my fellow applicants. One man could already have passed for a flight attendant based upon his demeanor, suit, and style; one woman was Chinese, and another was Latina. We chatted amiably all the way to the hotel where the interviews were being held.

Airline hiring requirements are strict. Height and weight must be proportionate, and you must be at least 5'2" tall (without shoes). The ability to speak a foreign language will inevitably move a candidate to the top of the interview list, and customer service work experience is highly desirable. I spoke Japanese and had about a year of retail work experience. I hoped both would stand me in good stead.

Frankly, I was intimidated by the interview process. While the interviewers were nice, I knew competition was stiff. Would the airline hire a 30-year-old man when more attractive, younger candidates were available? The next day I returned to the law firm, saying nothing to anyone about my application.

One afternoon the following week, I was working in my cubicle when my office phone rang. At best, office cubicles aren't private; at worst, everyone within earshot can easily overhear your conversations. TIA's language test proctor was phoning to ask if I could take a short language test right then and there! "Yes, I can," I answered, as I quickly set aside my legal work. For the next 15 minutes or so, the proctor engaged me in general airline-related conversation in Japanese. I was beyond nervous and self-conscious, speaking Japanese in my office! I only made one mistake by failing to use the correct linguistic register in asking a passenger to remain seated until the plane reached the arrival gate. Upon hanging up, I realized several colleagues were looking at me in wonderment. No one knew I could speak Japanese, and they were certainly surprised.

The rest of the hiring process moved at lightning speed. The airline conducted a background check covering the previous 10 years and made arrangements for me to fly to its Detroit airport medical clinic for my pre-hire physical exam. TIA offered me a training class slot in the second week of October, and I was ecstatic! When the offer came in a phone call to my office, my colleagues cheered me on, knowing I was overjoyed at being hired by the airline!

With only five weeks to plan, I had much to do in a very short time. In preparation for training, TIA instructed candidates to learn the airport codes for each of its destinations prior to arriving at the training center. On a personal level, I gathered quarters for washing machines during training, packed highlight markers and other study-related supplies, and packed my office clothes so I would be professionally dressed during training.

Wrapping up my affairs in Cleveland posed a challenge. I shared my apartment, and I felt my then-roommate was not unhappy at my departure! Failing the training wasn't an option, and I prepared for a major move after training. I intended to relocate to the city where I was assigned to a crew base. I hoped I'd be based in Detroit, a city with which I was at least minimally familiar and which had a cost of living similar to what I knew in Cleveland. I packed up my china, books, music, and video tapes, stacking everything in my room to await my return from training in late November.

~ ~ ~

Flight attendant training was a unique experience. I recognized five people from my initial interview in August; we'd all been hired! We were a diverse group representing several races, ages, genders, and sexual orientations. I didn't become friends with everyone; in fact, two individuals were very off-putting and never became friendly. Almost immediately, though, I became good friends with Lynn, a tall blonde Dutch woman, and Yvonne, a genteel French woman who was taking her first ever job outside her home. Lynn, Yvonne, and I formed an inseparable camaraderie that took us not only through the rigors of flight attendant training but stood for years to come.

Our training program was five weeks at TIA's vast training facility near the Minneapolis St. Paul airport. We were housed in comfortable corporate apartments furnished with all the necessities. I shared the apartment with two other male flight attendant trainees. We were a diverse bunch: I was the oldest, then came Miguel from San Juan, Puerto Rico (we'd met at the interview), and Bobby from Alabama who was just 22 years old and right out of college. We quickly became friendly and have remained so throughout our careers.

Six days a week, the training began **promptly** at 8:00 am, and tardiness was unacceptable. The very first day, one friendly trainee failed to return after our initial break. We were told he "elected to leave," and I was uncomfortable with the knowledge that training candidates were so expendable. Time didn't permit dwelling upon negative feelings; there was simply too much work to be done.

More than 75% of flight attendant training is purely academic. Trainees learn aircraft oxygen systems, how to extinguish fires, and how to check the working order of every piece of the aircraft's emergency equipment, as well as how to use the emergency equipment. First aid, CPR, and the use of Automated External Defibrillators (AEDs) are taught. Service training is exacting and precise. The operation of each aircraft door and window exit is covered, with strict attention paid to a rote command sequence. We learned to brief "able-bodied people" (called ABPs) to help us in an emergency evacuation. We learned how to both do and demonstrate the passenger brace position required in an emergency landing.

Emergency evacuation, the most critical aspect of training, is covered at length. Emergency commands are memorized verbatim. Each training candidate has to experience evacuating a plane via the emergency evacuation slide. In our training we used a 727 mock-up and slide for our exercise. Instructors led us through a simulated emergency landing. They briefed ABPs, demonstrated the brace position, and shouted commands, all while we heard the soundtrack of a simulated crash. The emergency slide was deployed, and each of us slid down. Since it was a simulation, we had grand fun! I watched Yvonne slide down in front of me; when my turn came, I jumped on the slide without a care in the world. In an instant I was on the ground laughing along with everyone else who had enjoyed their ride! We'd all have loved another go at it, but the instructors herded us right back to work. The twice-daily testing and the endless hours of studying were exhausting.

Saturday nights after training, several of us would go dancing in downtown Minneapolis, but eventually, Saturday night became the one night a week I could sleep as long as I wanted.

The academics were tough, and not everyone could keep up with the rigorous demands of the training. Several candidates either dropped out or failed out. My Dutch friend Lynn was struggling. English was her second language, and that made the training even more intense and challenging. Frustrated, she talked about quitting and returning to her job as a resort food and beverage manager in California. I made arrangements to meet with her after the day's training and worked with her one-on-one for several evenings. Thereafter, Lynn did a fine job depicting emergency procedures and persevered through the rest of the training.

One week before the end of training, we were given our base assignments. My class was evenly divided between Detroit and Boston.

Our class seniority, determined by age, dictated the order of choice. I was the tenth, and Yvonne and Lynn were immediately senior to me. We had no trouble holding Detroit. We began making preliminary arrangements.

Our final exam consisted of a one-on-one emergency preparation scenario with an instructor. Acting as a flight attendant on my assigned DC-10 aircraft, I had to depict every step for the instructor. Though nervous, I made it through with only one error of omission. On November 20, 1996, 30 new flight attendants graduated from training. We were all immensely proud to officially be flight attendants for TIA.

~ ~ ~

Becoming acclimated as a flight attendant is tough. You begin the job sitting on-call, waiting for Scheduling to contact you with a trip assignment. On December 1 our class went on-call; my first working flight took place on December 3. As an additional floater flight attendant, I worked several different flights with different crews. My very first layover was for 30 hours in Newark, New Jersey, giving me time to visit Manhattan and then take the train back to the hotel.

Over the next few years, my flying career was largely uneventful. Lynn and I shared a Detroit townhouse with another flight attendant, Russell, who was slightly senior to the two of us. Since Lynn and I were close in seniority, we often worked together and always had a good time. Lynn's son, Michael, was only eight years old when we started working for the airline, and he frequently visited us in Detroit. While initial flight attendant salaries are low, the travel benefits are an enormous opportunity. Using our flight passes, Lynn, Michael, Russell, and I went twice to Hawaii, to Cancun, Mexico, and to Arizona to see the Grand Canyon. Russell and I were romantically involved, and together we visited his friends in Portland, Oregon, his mother in Milwaukee, and my family in Ohio. On my own I visited friends in Germany, Los Angeles, New York City, and Toronto.

The Detroit crew base is dynamic and diverse. Being on-call, we can be assigned to any available open crew position. Flights depart daily to destinations all over the world: Amsterdam, Tokyo, Honolulu, London, Guam, Paris, Seoul, Singapore, Kansas City, Spokane, Lansing, Bismarck, Rochester, and Albuquerque, to name a few. Domestic trip sequences can be anywhere between one and five days, while international ones last three to eight days. Occasionally on-call flight attendants cover "unusual" flying for longer periods, such as extended intra-Asia trips between Tokyo and Bangkok, Manila, or Seoul, but those trips are rare. An on-call flight attendant may wake up in Detroit and go to bed anywhere in the TIA system.

While on call, I was able to visit Tokyo, Osaka, Nagoya, Seoul, Guam, Honolulu, Amsterdam, London, and Frankfurt many times. I constantly compared notes and learned from fellow flight attendants. Being very computer savvy, Lynn was instrumental in teaching me how to bid for trip sequences to avoid flights I detested, like all-night "red-eye" flights or those with extremely short overnights. The flight attendants and I worked most weekends and every holiday. As we gained seniority at the airline, we alternated between being on-call and having months when we were able to hold pre-determined schedules. We learned how and why the airline worked. We made new friends and learned which locations we liked or wished to avoid. I utilized my vacation time to go to Germany and to visit friends in Scotland. On a regular basis, Lynn flew to Amsterdam to be with her family, and Russell flew to Milwaukee to see his mother. In 1999 I took a two-day training course at headquarters in Minneapolis in order to join the airline's disaster response team, and in 2001 I trained to become a purser on international flights.

In time Russell, Lynn, and I each moved on. After five years together in the Detroit townhouse, we parted ways when the lease expired. We all became commuters to our Detroit crew base. Lynn bought a house in California; Russell returned home to Milwaukee and moved on to a new relationship; and I moved to Chicago. We each secured Detroit accommodations in crew member crash pads—apartments or hotel rooms shared by multiple crew members who spent a few nights there each month around trip sequence assignments.

The higher the time value of a trip, the fewer days I would have to work. As a commuter, I specifically wanted longer trips, so I often flew domestic five-day sequences because they were worth a lot of flight time. I averaged about 14 working days per month, picking up international trips whenever possible.

I left the Detroit crew base in November 2005 and started commuting to the crew base in New York City. At my seniority level, I was able to hold a better schedule there than in Detroit. Oh, how I loved New York City! Not only was the crew base good, I made new friends and held flight sequences with layovers that would have been impossible from Detroit. New York City itself was wonderful and fascinating. I particularly liked Ty's, a gay bar in Greenwich Village, and the Strand Bookstore at 12ᵗʰ and Broadway. But the commute from my Chicago home was complicated, taxing, and exhausting, leaving me with only a few days at home each month. In January 2008 I transferred back to the Detroit crew base.

By the time I returned to Detroit, hundreds of mostly senior flight attendants were retiring in response to an excellent retirement package TIA was offering. As a result, flight attendants around my seniority were suddenly able to hold better trip sequences. I began to hold an occasional Amsterdam flight, have good domestic layovers, and hold flights on the highly desirable Airbus 320/319 aircraft. Rather than having layovers in Bismarck and Saginaw, I held more desirable destinations—Orange County, California, and Phoenix, Arizona, to name a few. Over holidays I was able to hold Amsterdam and, sometimes, London. Asia was still too senior a destination for me to regularly bid and hold. When flight attendants want to trade trip sequences, they post on an "open" board on the computer scheduling system. So, when Asia trip sequences appeared on the "open" board, both Lynn and I would try to trade for them. Sometimes we succeeded!

~ ~ ~

My flight attendant career has been anything but mundane. On Saturday, January 2, 1999, a massive blizzard struck the US Midwest, paralyzing air traffic throughout the region. When I arrived at the airport for my assigned short domestic turnaround, a flight attendant asked if I would trade my trip for her high-value turnaround to St. Martin. I was happy to oblige, secretly hoping that I might get "stuck" in St. Martin overnight if the Midwest blizzard became severe enough. The flight from Detroit to St. Martin was uneventful, the crew members were nice, and we enjoyed the sun for the few minutes we were on the ground. The return flight was completely full. About half way to Detroit, while we were over Florida, we received word that, due to the storm, Detroit's airport was closed and we were diverting to Tampa.

Passengers and crew were provided with overnight accommodations, and at noon the following day we departed for Detroit. After an uneventful flight, we were met by complete chaos when we landed at Detroit Metro. Deep snow had buried the airport and surrounding areas. The airport had just re-opened, the snow had not been fully cleared, and they simply weren't prepared for the onslaught of inbound air traffic. In short order, 32 flights landed on the tarmac at Detroit Metro without the necessary gate space and without sufficient ground crew available to clear the snow. With nowhere to go, the planes formed a long line on the tarmac with passengers and crew stranded inside.

On each plane, food supplies had already been depleted by the in-flight cabin service. Now, the drinks ran out. Water tanks ran dry. Toilets filled up and began overflowing. The stressed-out passengers became angry. The control tower wasn't equipped to manage a problem of this magnitude. Pilots began requesting to take off and fly to any airport that could accept them, but permission was denied. Hours passed. On one airplane, a man claimed to have a heart attack. Rather than allow the plane to a gate to offload him, a catering truck was used to remove the passenger to a waiting ambulance. Some passengers called news outlets and gave live on-air accounts of what was happening.

For most of the ordeal I remained in the front galley with the purser attempting to assist her as passenger complaints escalated and the pilots continued to beg the control tower for information and direction. The airport was paralyzed, and nothing could be done. As nightfall approached, some of the passengers simply had had enough of the situation.

Aboard my flight a woman passenger in an exit row decided she was getting off the plane. At the beginning of our flight, per FAA regulations, I had briefed her and the other exit row passengers on the operation of the exits in the event of an evacuation. She knew the evacuation slide would automatically deploy if the door was opened. Braving the foul-smelling lavatory to change into winter clothes, she returned to her seat and told her husband of her plan. Passengers within earshot planned to join her in an escape down the slide. I was in the front galley with the purser when a sudden commotion erupted and a woman passenger shouted for a flight attendant. Thinking that a fight had broken out and I might need help, I quickly asked a hefty man seated in first class to come with me. We ran back to the site of the ruckus. In the moment it took us to arrive, the husband of the woman trying to escape had subdued her and was settling her back in her seat. We'd now been sitting on the tarmac for almost five hours, and nerves were definitely at the breaking point. I slumped in exhaustion on my jump seat next to the exit.

In the middle of the cabin, one passenger had an impressive idea and took action. He'd learned the name of TIA's CEO from the on-board magazine. Using his mobile phone, he called his cousin in suburban Minneapolis to learn the name of the most posh Minneapolis suburb. He placed a call to directory information and—amazingly—was given the CEO's home phone number. The CEO's wife answered, saying her husband was not available. Disbelieving, the passenger phoned again a few minutes later. This time the CEO himself answered. After the passenger explained the situation, the CEO asked to speak to the captain. The phone came forward to the captain, and the crew was awestruck that the CEO himself was on the line. At the same time, we were also miffed that it was necessary for a passenger to inform the CEO of a major problem occurring in Detroit. Promising to phone back, the CEO told the captain he'd make necessary arrangements to get everyone out of the mess.

Within an hour, we finally had movement. A skeleton crew had been cobbled together to dig out two aircraft gates. Each of the 32 planes was brought to a gate, offloaded, and then towed out of the way to make room for the next plane. Trash and checked luggage were left on board. Finally, seven hours and 25 minutes after landing, we were actually able to get off the plane! The airport was a madhouse, and the captain told us to remove crew identifiers from our bags and, if we could, change out of our uniforms before exiting the aircraft. Nothing could have prepared me for the pandemonium that was the terminal. Luggage was piled in corners to the ceiling. People occupied every inch of space, lying down or slumped over in chairs. Trash overflowed every receptacle, and every food concession was shut down due to lack of supplies. Total chaos.

The Blizzard of '99, as it became known, was well covered in both local and national news broadcasts, and *The Wall Street Journal* published a lengthy article about the fiasco. As a result of the event, a class-action lawsuit was filed against TIA. Attorneys representing the airline took statements from each crew member who was on one of the stranded planes. The airline lost the suit, and all affected passengers were provided with free tickets for future travel. The crew members, however, were simply paid for our time! This event, among others, triggered the creation of the Coalition for Airline Passenger's Bill of Rights. [NOTE: The Department of Transportation issued a final rule to enhance airline passenger protections that went into effect on April 29, 2010. See http://www.regulations.gov/#!documentDetail;D=DOT-OST-2007-0022-0262.]

~ ~ ~

On Monday, April 19, 1999, I was on the second day of a four-day domestic flight sequence, flying from Atlanta to Memphis, when our DC-9 developed a problem seconds after take-off. In an instant, the plane began filling with smoke. My jump seat was located between the two rear lavatories, and the lavatory smoke detectors were sounding. I called the captain on the intercom, using a specific emergency signal, and the captain said we would return to Atlanta. The other flight attendants and I felt an evacuation might be necessary after landing, so we began to make initial preparations. A bit shaken I stood at the over-wing exits and quickly briefed the passengers, and then I rushed back to my jump seat to brief the passengers near that exit door. We landed safely and, thankfully, an evacuation wasn't necessary.

~ ~ ~

Commercial air travel was redefined on September 11, 2001, particularly in the US. I had arrived at my commuter apartment in Detroit and collapsed, exhausted, into bed around midnight on September 10. I always fall asleep with talk radio playing. So, as I was waking up the next morning, I heard live coverage of the plane crash of American Airlines Flight 11 in New York City. Sitting up looking out at the beautifully warm day, I heard the radio announcer, via phone from New York City, suddenly begin shouting and screaming. The announcer in Windsor didn't know what was happening; I instantly knew, though, that it was something terrible. I rushed to wake up Russell, my ex-boyfriend and now roommate.

The horrors and devastation of 9/11 defied imagination. I cried - not only for the passengers and their families – but especially for my comrades, the 25 flight attendants lost aboard the four hijacked flights. I desperately wished I could have done something to help them - protected them, warned them, or gone in their stead. As a flight attendant myself, I knew the terror they faced as they valiantly attempted to get information to the ground and as they attempted to fight back on United Airlines Flight 93. Little did I know that my friend Jeffrey Collman was on that first plane, American Airlines Flight 11. Through interviews with his beloved partner, Keith Bradkowski, I would come to know more about Jeff as I researched his life for my first book, Jeff's Way.

Before 9/11 flight attendants were told to surrender and step back if our flight was ever hijacked. After 9/11 we were retrained in hijacking protocol and taught to fight back. Special classes were arranged to teach crew members strategic moves and responses. I joined a support group, The National Air Disaster Alliance. Through that group, I met the surviving siblings of Betty Ong, a flight attendant on the same flight with Jeff. Betty valiantly phoned the ground to report the hijacking in progress. The meetings of the Alliance were attended by many people who were affected in some way by an air disaster, and the experiences shared were profound.

~ ~ ~

In 1998, TIA began flying to India on DC-10 aircraft with Boston-based crews. The sequences were either seven or eight days long and operated via Amsterdam to either Mumbai or Delhi. The flight crews always made the most of their time in India by taking day trips to see the *Taj Mahal*—a white marble mausoleum built by Mughal emperor Shah Jahan in memory of his third wife—or the ancient city of Jaipur, both near Delhi. They shopped for clothes, carpets, ornaments, and even household appurtenances like granite which was a bargain in India compared to in the US! I know a flight attendant who even had new draperies custom-made in India.

By 2000, Detroit crews took over the India flights because Detroit's larger crew base could more easily handle the extended flight sequences. The trip sequences became six-day trips via Amsterdam with short 25-hour layovers in India. Flights arrived at midnight in India and departed 25 hours later at 1:00 am to return to Amsterdam. I preferred to work the Delhi flights rather than the Mumbai ones because Delhi is less of a madhouse than Mumbai. I found the shopping to be more interesting and the food delicious! After 9/11, TIA stopped flying to Delhi, ceding that route to another airline, so now Detroit crews only fly to Mumbai.

I didn't fly to Mumbai for many years. I wasn't opposed to it; at my seniority I simply wasn't able to hold the trip. The six-day sequences were worth a lot of flight time, so they were very popular. There were shops in the hotels in which the crew stayed, and crew members who regularly flew the route made friends with merchants who catered to the airline crews. The merchants became good at quickly fulfilling the crew's orders. You could be measured for a new outfit in the morning and have it delivered to you that night just before the crew's pick-up in the hotel lobby. Regular crew members networked, so merchants could easily send more complicated orders to the purchaser via another crew member. The TIA crew members were accommodated at the Trident-Oberoi Hotel at Nariman Point. Since numerous airlines frequently put their crews up at the same hotels, the Trident-Oberoi also had crew members from German International Airlines, French International Airlines, Alpine International Airlines from Switzerland, among others. The hotel afforded a crew hospitality room with food and drinks, computers available for crew use, and even a pool table.

The Trident-Oberoi Hotel is a five-star facility; in addition to a shopping arcade, its amenities include a luxurious health spa, beauty salon, barber shop, swimming pool, modern gymnasium, bars, numerous five-star restaurants, and a full-service travel agency. The lobby, domed by a gigantic atrium and glass walls that offer a stunning view of luxurious gardens, contains comfortable furniture, potted trees and plants, an orchid-filled fountain, and an elaborate front desk complex with a smaller private side desk specifically serving the needs of the air crews. The private desk staff arranges all the door keys for crew members, makes wake-up calls in preparation for crew departure, and answers any crew-related questions. By Western standards, the hotel is overstaffed, but it is the norm for Indian hotels catering to Westerners. Phone calls are answered *during* the first ring; housekeepers provide luxurious towels and sheets for the high, comfortable beds and stock the marble bathrooms with sweet-scented toiletry amenities. The service in the bars and restaurants is comparable to Maxim's in Paris. Indian staff members pride themselves on their quality of service, and it certainly shows. No request is too much to ask of them, and everyone speaks perfect English.

I enjoy Indian food. Although the hotel's restaurants offer wonderful fare, I usually prefer a short ride in a tuk-tuk cab (a three-wheeled auto rickshaw, the motorized version of the traditional pulled rickshaw or cycle rickshaw) to the Leopold Café and Bar, an eatery popular with foreign tourists and locals alike. Leopold's serves exotic curries, flavorful steamed rice, and wonderful naan at half the price it would cost at a hotel restaurant. The ambience of being out and about in Mumbai, meeting British, German, and Australian tourists, adds to the great experience of Leopold Cafe.

Mumbai is a beautiful, dynamic, exotic, noisy, congested, dirty, crowded, fascinating city. The streets are crammed with every imaginable wheeled vehicle: ox-drawn carts, luxury cars by *Mercedes-Benz*, tuk-tuk cabs, bicycles, buses, Toyotas, and push carts. Pedestrians weave in and out of the traffic. Street urchins beg for money, some cleaning windows for coins. Physically impaired people walk up to the cars and peer inside to see the occupants. The tuk-tuks swerve amid the hectic traffic...which can be more than terrifying! Women carry large bundles tied to their backs or large vases of water on top of their heads. Next to modern shopping arcades and designer stores, shantytown slums—complete with satellite television dishes perched on their roofs—occupy the space under road overpasses or in alleys. In some locations outside the main financial neighborhood, one must pass through shanties simply to enter a building. Roadside merchants sell sodas, candies, and crisps. Children rush up to tourists to sell "precious antiques" or plastic toys. At the old Mumbai International Airport urchins would clamor around inbound tourists and flight crews, begging for pens or pencils. The first few times I flew to India, I brought as many pens as I could to distribute. The children never physically touched anyone, and their poverty was heartbreaking to see.

Mumbai is filled with pollution, trash, and burning refuse in open barrels; dust and dirt; animals of every sort roaming freely; and elaborate houses of worship. High-tech glass high-rises, modern Western-style apartments, and endless high-rise slums are everywhere. People are everywhere. The weather is hot, humid, and steamy. India is a land of extremes and dichotomies.

~ ~ ~

Flight attendants frequently trade trip sequences or completely re-arrange our assigned monthly schedules by picking up open flights on the computerized scheduling "open board." Around 2000–2001, I was able to pick up a Mumbai trip sequence, as did a friend of mine, and we were happy to work together. In Mumbai he and I ventured out of the hotel to take a walk. We saw a street barber, the main train station, the TIA/NIA (Netherlands International Airlines) city ticket office, and numerous street vendors. I bought a small coin purse from one of them for pennies. Street food was readily available, but considering cleanliness and food safety regarding street food I preferred eating either the wonderful curry at Leopold Cafe or in the hotel.

I'm very active in the gay Leather community, so I frequently wear leather clothing. Custom-made clothing, leather or not, is much less expensive in Mumbai, so on one trip I planned to have some leather clothing made. I brought a pair of my well-fitted jeans and a uniform shirt that had a bit of a militaristic look and asked the merchant to make the two items in leather along with a leather vest. Unfortunately, I was never really happy with the results. The clothing was adequate. However, the quality of the leather was very poor, and the vest was too short. I made do with the items until I could afford to replace them, but I shied away from having anything else made on future overnight Mumbai layovers. Had I regularly flown the route, I might have felt differently.

Knowing flight crew members were a somewhat captive audience, the merchants in the hotel's shopping arcade actively courted us. They offered everything from Pashmina shawls to carpets to medicines to jewelry. I'm not much of a shopper, but occasionally I'll buy a few fun things to take home or as gifts. I bought a herd of small wooden ornamental elephants for a friend who always wanted to visit India but probably never will, along with some holiday ornaments for my mother. The merchants expected customers to bargain on the prices, something I abhor but force myself to do. For the elephants, I bargained the price down by about 40% of the original asking price...but I suspect I still paid more than their actual worth!

~ ~ ~

Flight attendant scheduling is anything but an exact science. Each month crew members bid for our preferred flight sequences and hope for the best. Seniority rules the award system; the longer flight attendants have been working for the airline, the better our chance of receiving our desired flight sequences, or at least tolerable ones. The computer scheduling program used by TIA in 2008 enabled flight attendants to enter variables in an attempt to specifically isolate exactly which trip sequences we hoped to be awarded.

When I bid for November 2008, I entered mostly negations into the bidding computer system (what I didn't want). I had just begun my 12th year of flying, which isn't very senior compared to many other flight attendants, so I couldn't be too picky. I wanted trip sequences departing after 12 noon, concluding by 8:00 pm, and flying internationally rather than domestically, if possible. I negated trip sequences of four days or fewer and listed my preferred sequences of at least five days, particularly longer international sequences. In order of preference I listed Saipan, Guam, Honolulu, and Amsterdam. I knew the long-haul Asian flights would probably be impossible for me to hold at my seniority, but I hoped for the best when I submitted my bid during the first week of October.

At that time I lived in Chicago and commuted to Detroit, TIA's largest crew base. My schedule for November 2008 was predictable. Early in the month I flew a five-day domestic sequence with my friend Jean. She was from New York City, and I appreciated her sarcastic sense of humor. I picked up an Amsterdam layover on November 19 and then had the Amsterdam-Mumbai-Amsterdam sequence departing Detroit on Sunday, November 23. This would be my first time in Mumbai since the summer of 2005. I'd be spending the Thanksgiving holiday flying, which I never minded. Immediately following that I was scheduled for a four-day domestic sequence that spanned the end of November and into December.

In early November my close friend Joanne Gaddy and I had an argument. We lived on the same street and were both very active in the gay Leather community. I took friendships seriously and felt that Joanne wasn't being as loyal a friend to me as she should have. Joanne and I were a lot alike - intelligent, articulate, outspoken, and forthright. The disagreement led to hurt feelings and several weeks during which we did not speak. Joanne became very irked with me. We truly did love each other, and she was exasperated at the estrangement. Joanne was not a person to let a situation go too long, so she determined to confront me about the matter as soon as she could.

On Saturday, November 22, 2008, I commuted from Chicago to Detroit to stay overnight before flying out on Sunday. While there I phoned my friend Orlando Sherman, a fellow flight attendant, and made plans to meet for dinner that night. Orlando's flight time report on Sunday was earlier than mine, so I dropped him back at the hotel immediately after dinner. I then headed out to the Detroit Eagle, a gay Leather bar that was having its annual "Mr. Detroit Eagle" contest. I enjoyed the contest, had a drink with friends, and then went back to the hotel.

The following morning, I turned on my computer and signed into Yahoo Chat. Almost immediately, Joanne sent me a message, and we began speaking about the estrangement. Being her usual forthright self, Joanne said, "I want to remain friends, but we need to work this out. Or, if you want to end our friendship, then just say so. It's your call." We spoke back and forth, eventually agreeing to resolve the matter and remain friends. I told her when I'd be back in Chicago after my upcoming round of flying to Amsterdam and Mumbai, and we made a plan to meet and talk upon my return. We ended the Chat by telling each other "I love you."

~ ~ ~

Prior to the departure of any trip sequence, the crew meets for a briefing. Domestic crew briefings are held in the inflight offices at designated briefing tables, while international crew briefings are held in designated briefing rooms also in the inflight offices. The designated "A" flight attendant domestically, or purser internationally, generally talks with the other flight attendants about service expectations; addresses FAA mandated safety matters—such as making sure passengers seated in the plane's exit rows are briefed before closing the boarding door; mentions the anticipated flying time; and covers any expected turbulence while in flight. Other matters are also covered, such as the number of special meals needed (Kosher or vegetarian) or passengers with special need (children flying alone). International crew briefings usually last about 15 minutes.

During these briefings a bid sheet detailing all flight attendant work positions is distributed; flight attendants sign up, in order of seniority, for their desired work positions on the plane. Each position is delineated by a crew member jump seat along with specific work details assigned to that seat.

Only a minority of TIA's Detroit-based crew members actually live in metro Detroit. The beauty of working for an airline means you are able to live anywhere you chose, as long as you are able to commute, using your free flight privileges, to your assigned crew base. Since my philosophy is that I have to work no matter who my fellow flight attendants might be, I don't usually pay attention to the published crew list when I check in for my flights.

~ ~ ~

On Sunday November 23, 2008, at 4:30 pm, our crew briefing began in a briefing room in the Detroit Inflight offices. I soon discovered that I was relatively junior, number six out of eight flight attendants. When the bid sheet reached me, I was disappointed. I wanted to work in business class, but other more senior flight attendants had already chosen those positions. Further, no senior flight attendants chose to work the duty free cart meaning I'd have to do it; I despised having to work the duty free cart. (Working the duty free cart usually falls to the junior flight attendants because the job is cumbersome and senior crew members tend to avoid it) Resigned to working in the main cabin, I had three positions from which to choose along with the duty free cart: work the main cabin galley, which I immediately passed as I wasn't comfortable with that work at the time; work a service cart in the main cabin aisle and assist passengers with carry-on luggage during boarding, sitting in a jump seat behind the wing; or work a service cart in the main cabin aisle and greet passengers at the plane's boarding door, sitting in a rear cabin jump seat. I chose the last position.

The flight attendants on my crew that day represented a mix of junior and senior crew members, races, ages, and genders. I had previously flown with two of them, Mary McAlister and Paula Burns. Both women commuted from their homes to the Detroit crew base: Mary from Charlotte, North Carolina, and Paula from Manchester, New Hampshire. Mary and Paula, both 58 years old, were old friends. They had flown for Pan Am prior to its bankruptcy. When Pan Am closed its doors, both of them started all over again as new hires for TIA in 1992 with Paula being senior to Mary by one week. Mary's shoulder-length dark hair was pulled back into a tight ponytail; while Paula's curly auburn hair was bobbed at chin length. As we gathered for the flight, Paula showed off her favorite earrings she chose to wear to celebrate the Thanksgiving holiday; Mary chuckled, remembering when Paula bought them in Mumbai a year before. Mary had originally been scheduled to work this trip sequence leaving a day later. Upon learning that Paula was flying the same trip sequence departing the day before, Mary managed to trade her flight for this one, allowing them to work together.

Tony Park from Portland Oregon, a 33-year-old second-generation Korean American, spent much of the month of November on vacation in New Zealand and Australia. He'd returned to the US only two days earlier and commuted to Detroit for this trip sequence. Posting on the "open board," Tony had tried for weeks to give away this trip, so he could enjoy more time off. No one took him up on it, so here he was.

Juan Lopez, 39, commuted to Detroit from his home in Miami. He had just worked a three-day Paris trip sequence that ended on Saturday, November 22, so he stayed overnight at a hotel near the Detroit airport.

David Johnson, 36, commuted from Dallas that Sunday morning. Not originally assigned to our flight, David traded an assigned domestic trip sequence for a position on our flight.

Colleen Ballard, 48, commuted into Detroit that morning from her home in Philadelphia. The most senior flight attendant on our crew, Colleen had been flying for TIA for 25 years. She was originally scheduled to be off over the Thanksgiving holiday, but she decided she'd rather take Christmas and New Year's off to spend with her family. That way, her husband and two teen-aged children could visit her in-laws for Thanksgiving...without her. Colleen traded a three-day Tokyo sequence for the six-day Mumbai trip over Thanksgiving. This would be Colleen's second Mumbai visit, and she excitedly planned to do holiday shopping in Mumbai.

My biggest surprise that day, however, was Nicolas Dumont walking into the briefing room as our purser. Nicolas, 45 years old, had upgraded to purser only six months before after having worked as a flight attendant for 24 years. Several years earlier, I had gone on a date with him, just one date, and it was a disaster. Seeing him made me uncomfortable.

Nicolas and I had been acquainted for a number of years. We didn't really know each other until a couple of years previously when I'd looked at him in a different light. He was attractive, tall with dark blonde hair and a solid build. He was born in the US to French Canadian parents and spoke fluent English and French. As we occasionally flew together, I eventually took an interest in him.

He lived in St. Louis but came to Chicago to see me when I asked him out. I had hoped that we'd have sparks that would lead to more dates; sadly, though, we didn't gel. Opposites may attract, but they don't always make it in the long run. I was very forthright, sexually open, liberal, and could sometimes appear forward. Nicolas was more private and more conservative. I felt Nicolas didn't give me a fair chance to show him who and what I was. After that failed experience, I tended to avoid him, going out of my way not to engage him if we crossed paths at the crew base.

That day in Detroit, it seemed that Nicolas was making an effort, albeit slightly forced, to be welcoming to me. "Good to see you, Doug. Glad you're back in Detroit. You were based in New York City, weren't you?" "Yes," I replied noncommittally, "I've been back since January." "Great!" he chirped and began his crew briefing.

We were assigned to work one of TIA's relatively new A330 Airbus airplanes. With a capacity of 298 passengers, our flight to Amsterdam that Sunday evening left Detroit with 21 open seats. Nicolas, Colleen, and Juan would work in business class; Mary, Paula, Tony, David, and I would work the main cabin, Tony managing the galley and the rest of us working the twin aisles.

Walking to the departure gate for our flight, I fell into step with Colleen, whom I'd not previously met. A petite 5'6" with blonde hair tied in a neat bun, Colleen was cheerful and friendly, with an air of competence and integrity about her. We discussed our commutes. "I'm not originally from Philadelphia," Colleen pointed out, "but I've lived there now for 20 years. I was raised in Ohio." "I'm from Ohio, too!" I enthused, "Where in Ohio are you from?" It turned out that Colleen and I had grown up only an hour's drive apart, with me a few years behind her. Colleen was from Cleveland's eastern suburbs, and I'm from Ashtabula, a small city in Ohio's extreme northeast corner, midway between Cleveland and Erie, Pennsylvania. We commiserated about growing up in the Snow Belt.

Colleen's 18-year-old daughter, Lisa, was home from college for Thanksgiving. Colleen had hoped Lisa could fly standby for the Mumbai trip. Although there was room on the flight to Amsterdam, the flight from Amsterdam to Mumbai was completely full. Disappointed,

Colleen told her daughter that, on her next vacation from school, they'd either go to Seoul or to Beijing.

Upon boarding the plane, flight attendants first stow their luggage and then check all emergency equipment in the vicinity of our assigned jump seat. Oxygen bottles and fire extinguishers must be full; flashlights must be in place; the jump seat must be in operational order; and the public-address microphone must be working.

My jump seat for the entire sequence was at the rear left-hand side door. TIA's catering supervisor and Tony checked the galley to ensure all necessary items were in place: all the meals, the trays in the carts, the fully-stocked beverage carts, and all the morning light-breakfast food and drinks for the Amsterdam pre-arrival service.

At the boarding door, I greeted incoming passengers and directed them towards their seats. In business class Nicolas and the catering representative checked that galley to ensure all supplies were present and ready for service. After Nicolas and Colleen prepared and served the pre-departure beverages to their business class passengers, Nicolas made routine boarding announcements directing passengers to correctly stow carry-on luggage, stow electronic equipment, be seated, and fasten seatbelts. Mary joined Juan, Nicolas, and Colleen as they served pre-departure drinks and hung up coats. David, Paula, and Tony worked in the main cabin, helping passengers get settled and closing the luggage bins.

During a pause in the boarding process, David stopped at the boarding door to exchange pleasantries with me. When he and I realized we'd previously met and worked together, David said "I remember you." I replied, "I hope I was nice and that's why you remember me." "No, not at all," a poker-faced David responded. I look askance at David, and then I realized he was joking! We had a chuckle, and David quickly returned to the main cabin.

The flight to Amsterdam was largely uneventful. With such a small staff and so many passengers, we were busy. We managed the initial beverage service, then the meal/beverage combination, followed by the duty-free cart that offered items for sale. The meal/beverage carts we used on the flight were poorly designed. In order to reduce staffing levels and costs, TIA had redesigned the meal service carts. A few bottled beverages were located on top of each cart, allowing one flight attendant to simultaneously serve the meal and offer one of the select drinks. One flight attendant served the main cabin from front to rear; another flight attendant worked from rear to front; they met in mid-cabin. On a full A330 Airbus with 264 passengers in the main cabin, this plan made for ineffective service: it took far too long to serve a meal and a beverage, especially since passengers invariably wanted a drink that wasn't available on the cart.

Mary and I worked the right-hand side aisle. She began with her cart at the front of the cabin working aft, while I began at the back working forward. Tony hurried to prepare a second cart for me to use when my first one was empty. Mary and I eventually met in the center of the cabin. On the left-hand side of the cabin, Paula and David did the same.

Selling duty-free items was, to say the least, not my favorite position. At that time, pages of paperwork were involved, and credit card payments were run on the old-fashioned imprinting machines that were definitely not user friendly. In addition, we accepted cash payments. If we were handed a $100 bill for a $30 purchase, we were expected to somehow find change, since we were not provided with a cash bank. Even though commissions were paid to the flight attendant working the duty-free cart, I never went out of my way to make sales. David worked with me on our flight, and he was the only one who did any talking. A tall, suave African-American with a shaved head, David was definitely a "ladies man." Women easily fell under his spell, and he'd sell hundreds of dollars' worth of perfumes and jewelry by charming and complimenting the ladies. His sales ability was both phenomenal and entertaining. I simply assisted him as best I could. David routinely earned several hundred dollars' worth of commissions from duty-free sales every year. I had to hand it to him; he knew how to close a sale!

Once the main service was complete and the duty-free cart put away, we could enjoy a short crew rest break. I spent the quiet lull back in the rear galley until Nicolas called me from the front to ask if I'd help Juan who was assisting an amputee who needed to use the lavatory. Juan had gotten the aircraft's on-board wheelchair, and together we helped the woman onto the chair and down the aisle to the lav. A bit uncomfortable with the process, Juan was surprised that she didn't have a traveling companion to assist her. I, however, knew that having a travel companion was not absolutely necessary since the Americans with Disabilities Act required crew members to reasonably assist disabled passengers. Once we had her back in her seat, I returned to the galley to begin preparations for the Amsterdam pre-arrival breakfast service while Tony took his crew break.

~ ~ ~

We arrived in Amsterdam at about 8:00 am on a cold, gloomy Monday. Exhausted, we made our way through Schiphol Airport to the waiting crew bus that would take us to the crew hotel across the Grand Canal from Amsterdam's Central Station.

After checking into my room, I phoned my friend Ronald, a local Dutch man with whom I'd become great friends as I flew to Amsterdam over the years. We agreed to meet in the evening at the Cuckoo's Nest bar, a popular local gay bar. Ronald phoned his friends Arjen and Leo, letting them know I was in town, and they decided to join us. Both of them had also become my friends. The four of us had an enjoyable evening over Heineken beers. "I wish I could stay later," I told them, "but I have to fly to Mumbai tomorrow. I'll be back Thursday morning, so shall we meet again Thursday evening?" Leo and Arjen wouldn't be free to meet, so Ronald and I made plans for me to phone him when I arrived. Hugging and kissing everyone goodbye, I made my way through Amsterdam's boisterous nightlife back to the hotel.

Mary and Paula invited everyone on the crew to join them for snacks when we arrived at the hotel in Mumbai. In preparation, they spent their Amsterdam layover shopping. They bought cold cuts, bread, cheese, potato chips, crackers, and a few small envelopes of condiments. Generous as well as thoughtful, they didn't even ask us for contributions toward the food.

~~~

In Detroit on Monday, November 24, the crew for TIA's regularly scheduled daily Amsterdam-Mumbai-Amsterdam sequence checked in for their trip, one day behind my crew. Among the eight flight attendants were Anne Fitzsimmons, who had traded with Mary on my flight, Debra Welch, and Samantha King. Debra and Samantha were my friends; over the years, we had often worked together. A Metro-Detroit native, Samantha was strikingly beautiful with runway model good looks, ebony skin, and perfectly coiffed hair. She was elegant, eloquent, and regal. I had always thought Samantha and Diahann Carroll could have been twins! Anne, in contrast, was a full four inches shorter than Samantha, had long blonde hair she wore up in a clip, and preferred uniform trousers to the uniform dresses worn by Samantha. Hailing from Pittsburgh, Anne exhibited a quiet confidence that drew people to her, just as people were drawn to Samantha's outgoing personality. Debra was from Des Moines, Iowa; she exhibited a quiet graciousness. Her grandmother, a Native American from a Colorado Cheyenne tribe, taught her to be strong. "The ancestors gave you that strength," her grandmother would solemnly intone.

On the flight to Amsterdam that Monday night, Samantha worked the rear main cabin galley while Anne and Debra worked together in the aisle. They arrived in Amsterdam on Tuesday, November 25, as my crew was leaving Amsterdam to fly to Mumbai.

TIA's flights to Mumbai left at 10:25 am to allow passengers arriving in Amsterdam early in the morning, connecting from all over the globe, to continue on to Mumbai without too long of a layover.

Tuesday morning saw the usual hubbub in the hotel's lobby. Crews in the process of checking in and out crossed paths. I didn't see Samantha, Anne, or Debra, but I did happen to meet my flight attendant friend, Jessica Thompson, who was checking out to fly to

Washington, DC. She was on a six-day trip sequence that went back and forth to Washington, DC via Amsterdam. She was also scheduled to arrive back in Detroit on Friday. Coincidentally, she was working her trip sequence with my good friend Lynn. Their sequence departed Detroit on November 23rd also, about an hour after mine did.

"Doug!" Jessica called, seeing me in the lobby and rushing over to hug me. "Hi, honey. Where are you going today?" "Mumbai," I told her. "We're returning here on Thursday morning." "Me, too!" Jessica enthused. "The hotel's throwing us a Thanksgiving buffet Thursday. Let's meet and go together. I haven't seen you in ages! I'm flying with Lynn. She's at her parents' house now, but I'll ask her to join us when we return!" "Wonderful," I responded, deciding to cancel with Ronald when I returned. "I look forward to joining you Thursday." "Safe trip, hon; see you when we get back." We hugged again and then scurried to our respective crew buses for the ride back to Schiphol Airport.

On the bus to the airport, we met the pilots who were taking us back and forth on the India leg of our journey. The captain, Daniel Abbott, 55, was from Phoenix, Arizona, and had been a captain for 12 years. Thoughtful and kind, Captain Daniel made Mumbai his usual route. I recognized him, remembering I'd flown with him to Mumbai years ago. The first officer, Sam Wilson, 52, was a former Navy pilot from Baltimore, Maryland. He joined TIA 20 years ago, after retiring from the Navy. I recognized Sam, too, because we'd flown back and forth from Amsterdam several times before. Ian Reid, 49, from Westchester, New York, was the second officer, and the only pilot I had not previously met. The first and second officers occupy identical roles on the flight deck. "First" or "second" simply designates who takes the first crew break. Extended overseas flights usually exceed eight hours of flying time, so the planes are staffed by three pilots to ensure that two pilots will always be on duty on the flight deck at all times, regardless of scheduled crew breaks.

Our plane from Amsterdam to Mumbai was an Airbus 300–200. This smaller plane accommodated an equal number of passengers in business class but, fortunately, 50 fewer in the main cabin. We each filled the same work positions that we had filled on our Detroit to Amsterdam flight, since the configuration of the plane was identical, with the exception of the main cabin size. Again, I worked the boarding door welcoming the Mumbai-bound passengers.

About the time we arrived at Schiphol Airport to fly to Mumbai, TIA's inbound Detroit flight carrying Samantha, Anne, and Debra arrived. We didn't see each other, though. Anne, in particular, was exhausted and wanted only to go to the hotel and get some sleep.

In the Netherlands International Airlines' offices at Schiphol Airport, TIA crews were briefed for outbound flights, just as we'd been prior to our Detroit departure. Two Netherlands International managers, Douwe and Alex, usually met and briefed the outbound crews. Today we were briefed by Douwe who was informal and friendly since he had met many of us over the years. Nicolas, Paula, and Mary, in particular, joked with Douwe as we were briefed. Having flown through Amsterdam many times, they had come to know Douwe and his fellow managers well. Snow flurries were falling in Amsterdam that morning, and Douwe tried to teach us how to pronounce the Dutch word for snow. Only Mary came close to the correct pronunciation much to everyone's delight. We made our way to the departure gate.

~ ~ ~

Regina Schumann, a German International Airlines' flight attendant, kissed her husband Lutz goodbye and made her way to Frankfurt Main Airport in a light drizzle on Monday, November 24. On a spacious Boeing 777 aircraft, Regina was the purser on the first of GIA's two daily flights to Mumbai. This flight offered a longer layover in Mumbai, arriving at 11:00 pm, with crew pick-up for the return flight at 2:00 am, 26 hours later. The second daily departure to Mumbai had a shorter layover—20 hours—arriving at 2:00 am, with crew pick-up at midnight the following night. Regina always preferred the longer layover whenever she could have it.

Regina, capable and professional, had been a GIA flight attendant for 21 years as of November, 2008; she had been a chief purser since July

2006. Joining her on the crew for GIA's first flight to Mumbai that day were Katrin Sammler, the second purser, who was very friendly yet brooking no nonsense; Nina Hoffman, the junior flight attendant, with a happy, bubbly personality; Barbara Weiler; Monika Klouse; Heike Muller; Christiane Schmidt; Elisa Rau; Angelica Sebastian; and Sandy Lutmann. Regina knew she had a good crew, and they all looked forward to a smooth flight.

~ ~ ~

On Tuesday afternoon in Mumbai, as the TIA and GIA flights prepared to leave Europe, a couple from Lagos, Nigeria—Ladi and Fola Sheyabu—were concluding a day of meetings with Indian Oil International executives and were preparing to join them for dinner. At 41, Ladi was Nigerian Oil Consolidated's senior sales specialist; his wife, Fola, also 41, was the attorney overseeing contract compliance for the sales agreements between Nigerian Oil and Indian Oil. Indian Oil wanted to buy oil to supply its expanding economy, and Nigerian Oil recognized the opportunity for a lucrative sale that offered a tidy profit. The Sheyabus, complementary professionals, were a remarkable team and frequently made joint business trips. This was their second visit to Mumbai in 2008. At 7:00 pm Tuesday evening, they were seated in the elegant Indian restaurant in the lobby of their hotel, the Trident-Oberoi. They were looking forward to the following day when they would have a few hours of free time in the late afternoon.

~ ~ ~

The Trident-Oberoi Hotel in Nariman Point, Mumbai, was one of the finest five-star hotels in Mumbai; it catered to an extensive international clientele. It was actually two hotels joined by a linked lobby with a common shopping arcade, outdoor pool, and spa. The Trident side consisted of a 30-story tower, and the Oberoi side was a smaller 18-story tower. The twin hotels catered to every conceivable guest need. The health spa conveyed the utmost in luxury, with a massage therapist, wet and dry saunas, and a full gymnasium. The beauty salon provided full service, including hair stylists, nail manicurists, and cosmetics consultants. In the lobby, three restaurants and two bars were ready to please the palates of their guests. On the mezzanine level, two dining rooms could accommodate large crowds or provide a more intimate private dining experience. Both rooms could be easily converted to business meeting space. Although the pool's main entrance was on the other side of the building, the outdoor pool could be accessed from the mezzanine by a single door. Visible from the pool level, stunning gardens flanked the back of the hotel.

To most of the hotel's foreign guests, the most attractive feature was the shopping arcade, which offered almost everything. A few shops in particular carried very popular products: carpets, leather goods, medicines, and jewelry. Although prices had, of course, risen over the years, skillful bargaining—common in Indian culture—could result in very good deals. My personal favorites were the arcade's bookstore, the art shop with beautiful, inexpensive, Indian picture prints, and a shop selling every sort of Indian ornament.

Located on Marine Drive, the Trident-Oberoi sat in the heart of the downtown financial district. Within blocks were the Taj Mahal Hotel, Leopold Cafe, a branch of CitiBank, and a multi-level shopping mall complex. From the front of the hotel, there was a stunning view of the beach front along the Indian Ocean known as "The Queen's Necklace." The Trident-Oberoi was the best of the best in India.

India's tropical climate meant that the November weather was warm and clear. Summer was the rainy season, but winter was an ideal time to visit. After the dreary winter cold of both Chicago and Amsterdam, I welcomed a day in tropical Mumbai.

~ ~ ~

On the plane I greeted the Mumbai-bound passengers as they boarded. Aside from a few Dutch passengers, the majority began their journeys far from Amsterdam. Most were coming from the US, some from Canada, and a few from other places. Nicolas made all the luggage announcements he could, but numerous pieces of luggage had to be checked at the boarding door since the plane's cabin simply could not accommodate everything. The Netherlands International gate agents managing our flight were wonderful. Standing in the jet bridge by the boarding door, they were prepared for the last-minute luggage checks. One passenger became quite irate at being told he had to check his bag, and he began to argue. The gate agent quietly, authoritatively, and unflinchingly, told the passenger, "Don't make this harder on yourself. Arguing with me will simply create a greater problem for you." Still fuming, the man surrendered his luggage to the agent and boarded the plane.

With everyone boarded we were ready to depart. Our anticipated flight time was eight hours and 30 minutes, with our scheduled landing in Mumbai a few minutes before midnight on November 25.

The crew worked hard on the flight. Passengers seemed to be more on the needy side than usual, and they walked around the cabin. The flight attendant call lights were pressed, sometimes four or five of them lighting up at the same time. Some passengers accidentally pressed the call lights, while others wanted something specific. We had to try to keep the passengers from congregating in the galley. This was dangerous because under any circumstances there were many carts and hot racks of entrees moving about in a very small space. It was trying to conduct the beverage and meal services under such conditions, and we had to instruct the passengers to clear the aisles so we could proceed.

If passengers want multiple drinks with their meal, service flow is disrupted and slowed. Meals themselves are sometimes difficult, with as many as one-third of the entrees being special meals required for cultural, religious, or health reasons. Special meals, like vegetarian, are not always very appetizing. Sometimes not all the requested special meals are boarded. This, understandably, irritates passengers who have made their meal requirements in the proper manner, and they sometimes take it out on the flight attendants—even though we have absolutely no control over what meals are boarded.

I began meal service working my way forward from the rear right-side door, and Mary began from the forward galley, shared by the main cabin and business class. In the left-hand aisle, Paula began in the front, while David worked from the back. Tony worked in the galley, frequently checking on us and bringing us replenishments as needed. Service was designed so the carts would meet at the cabin's half-way point, at the third cabin doors behind the wings. As I was nearing Mary in the aisle, I was hiding my growing exasperation with complaints about the meal choices and the multiple drink demands. I could barely keep up! Our supplies were running low. The situation was very frustrating for the passengers and for the flight attendants.

At the door three exit row, right behind the wings, two Dutch men were requesting drinks while four or five other passengers were calling for third and fourth drinks. Even Kali, the Indian god with all the arms, couldn't have kept up! Now right in front of Mary, I threw up my hands in despair, shouting "JUST A MINUTE!" to the clamoring passengers. Mary, handing me her remaining entrees, looked irked at my outburst, but I was too frustrated to care. When I finally finished the service and pulled the cart back into the rear galley, I joined David to begin the duty-free service.

Most of a flight from Amsterdam to Mumbai takes place during the daylight hours, with dusk falling as planes near the Indian Ocean. The on-board video entertainment isn't enough to keep everyone seated and quiet. As David and I pushed the duty-free cart through the cabin, we were constantly faced with passengers milling around the cabin. One elderly woman kept poking me in the back demanding we move the cart out of her way. Finally, she poked me one time too many and got quite snippy with me. I lost my temper and, in front of everyone, I shouted at her that I'd have her arrested for assault if she touched me again. She stalked off closing herself in a lavatory.

The constant demands, unending service, and tight quarters all combined to result in the crew's complete exhaustion. By the time we finally landed in Mumbai, I was completely wrung out and looking forward to a beer in the crew lounge.

Upon entry into India, every crew member had to declare each electronic device being brought in, as well as perfumes and tobacco. In addition, we had to fill in a form with our passport information and show our crew IDs to the customs officers. In 2008, the agent meeting the flight escorted the crew through the crowds in the arrivals hall to the crew bus. The Mumbai airport at the time was rudimentary and the parking lot was just outside of the terminal building. I had brought about 20 pens with me to distribute to the children I expected to have begging outside the terminal building, and I was disappointed there were none. I thought that was odd.

We climbed up into the old bus while our luggage was piled into the belly storage compartments. The Trident-Oberoi Hotel was far from the airport, all the way downtown in Mumbai's financial district, but we were there in about 30 minutes. Foreign faces meant money to impoverished street people. It was common—and nerve-wracking—to have people walk directly up to the bus and peer in the windows. To avoid that attention, the bus driver and assistants encouraged us to keep the bus curtains drawn. I discreetly looked out on the teeming mass that was Mumbai; unimaginable poverty greeted me wherever I looked.

~ ~ ~

Upon arrival at the Trident-Oberoi Hotel, we were happily welcomed by familiar faces. At the front door, a tall, jovial, gentleman host in an elaborate tunic and turban was the first to greet each incoming crew member. Our keys, prepared by Najeema, a lovely and gracious woman, were waiting for us at her desk in a quiet corner of the lobby. My room was 1609. Since I tend to prefer odd-numbered rooms, I was content with my room assignment.

Captain Abbott made frequent trips to Mumbai, so he was a regular guest at the Hotel and received warm greetings from the employees. The Captain had brought a case of Heineken from Amsterdam for the Mumbai layover, and the staff hurried to take the beer to the upstairs crew lounge and put it on ice.

The Hotel had a hospitality lounge for crew members on the fourth floor, and Captain Abbott invited us to meet there in 30 minutes for drinks. Any and all flight crew members were welcome in the lounge; on any given night, there would be crews from TIA, German Air International, Alpine International, South African, Aeroflot, and others. By the time I arrived in the lounge, Mary and Paula had laid out their snack spread and pulled chairs and tables together. Nicolas, Juan, Ian, Sam, and Captain Abbott joined Mary, Paula, and me. I was disappointed that Colleen and Tony weren't there. Across the room, several South African crew members were shooting pool, and we invited two pilots from German International Airlines to join us.

We laughed and enjoyed ourselves; around 3:00 am, I decided to go to bed. Juan and I took the elevator together. I exited on the 16th floor, and he continued up to his room on the 18th floor, near Nicolas. With the television tuned to BBC news, I drifted off to sleep.

Unfortunately, jet lag awakened me early on Wednesday, November 26, after only about six hours of sleep. Looking out at the brilliant sunshine of a tropical Mumbai morning, the street below swarmed with every form of wheeled and human traffic. I hoped I'd run into other crew members who'd join me for a meal at Leopold Cafe, a short tuk-tuk ride from the Hotel. Meanwhile, I decided to visit the shopping arcade that was just opening for the day.

When the elevator arrived on my floor, I was delighted to see Colleen, who was also heading to the arcade. I invited Colleen to dine with me at Leopold Cafe later that day, but she said she preferred to stay in and order room service. Since it was still early, not even 11:00 am, Colleen and I had the shopping arcade to ourselves. I felt like I was coming down with a mild cold, so I wanted to buy some cough drops and cold medicine. Colleen wanted herbal teas and the sleep aids that were popular among crew members. At the chemist's shop, I quickly bought my items, while Colleen took longer to speak with the pharmacist. While waiting for her, I walked through the hall of shops.

Shopping in India is a fascinating cultural experience that can also be overwhelming or off-putting. As you near a shop, the merchant will stand at the entrance calling out, "Hello, sir; come in, take a look!" You'll hear the same refrain at every shop you pass, and some merchants get a bit insistent. "SIR! Come in! What do you want? I have everything! Come in, come in!"

When Colleen completed her transaction, she and I walked back to the lobby, meeting Mary, Paula, and Nicolas as they headed toward the arcade. We chatted for a few minutes. Paula wanted to visit the jewelry shop, Nicolas sought the textile merchant to have new curtains custom-made for his home, and Mary hoped to buy a purse she'd seen on a previous trip.

Colleen decided to return to her room, so I joined the others, asking if anyone was interested in going out for Indian food for lunch. "Go to Trishna's Restaurant; it's new," said Nicolas. "I went to Leopold Cafe last time and got sick from something I ate." Mary and Paula agreed to join me after they finished their shopping. Paula went off to the jewelry shop, while I went with Mary. As we walked toward one of the shops, an Indian woman wearing western-style clothes walked by us and said, "I hope you're bargaining!" We assured her we were. Happily, Mary found and bought her purse, and then we went around the corner to the book store. I bought a handful of postcards, some to send from Mumbai and some to take home. Next, we went to the art and print shop where I purchased some Indian picture prints as gifts. Having completed our shopping, Mary and I rejoined the others.

In the textile shop, Nicolas and Paula visited with the owner, Amil. We had all come to know him over numerous trips to Mumbai. Amil graciously offered us tea and soft drinks as we chatted. In western cultures, we were accustomed to simply walking in and buying what we wanted. In India I had come to learn that shopping was a more elaborate experience. Indian merchants preferred a more personal relationship with customers, spending time chatting and visiting. This type of relationship enabled the merchant to understand you as a person, to learn your needs and wants, to gauge your personality, and to assess your bargaining skills, all with the goal of successfully managing a transaction with you.

Nicolas and Paula spoke to Amil about several new items, such as shirts and suits, which he had recently added to his inventory. Paula asked about reproducing a jacket she'd seen in a magazine and said she would bring a picture on her next trip to Mumbai the first week in December, at which time they could discuss the price.

We moved on to Mr. Gupta's jewelry shop, where Paula browsed his collection of rings, bracelets, and necklaces. Ever gracious, Mr. Gupta was warm and welcoming, heartily shaking hands with each of us. "So lovely to see you again, Paula," he gushed, "Please, everyone, sit down." A shop assistant offered tea or soft drinks and, having learned that it was culturally inconsiderate to refuse refreshments, I again enjoyed a bottle of cola.

Paula had her eyes on a lovely necklace, and she tried it on. It was beautiful, and the simple design suited her perfectly and complemented her coloring. "I'll offer a special price just for you, Paula! After all, the necklace is a perfect match to the earrings you bought from me." Paula chuckled to herself, knowing those were her favorite earrings. After a few minutes of perfunctory bargaining, Paula handed Mr. Gupta her credit card and wore the necklace out of the shop.

Preparing for our lunch excursion, we entered the bustling hotel lobby around 2:00 pm. Nicolas declined in favor of taking a nap. We saw David in the lobby and invited him to join us. He accepted, and the jovial turbaned man at the front door hailed a tuk-tuk cab for us, telling the driver to take us to Trishna's Restaurant. The four of us crowded into the tiny cab, me in front next to driver and David, Paula, and Mary scrunched together in the back seat.

Driving in Mumbai was an adventure unto itself! Tuk-tuks were insubstantial, open, three-wheeled vehicles lacking both doors and seatbelts. You got in and held onto a pole for dear life, while whizzing all around you were bicycles, busses, private cars, and pedestrians.

The tuk-tuk drivers careened around everything, rarely slowing down and only when they could not get around an obstruction. Hot, humid, fetid, pollution-clogged air assaulted our nostrils and embedded itself into our clothing. The drive from the Trident-Oberoi Hotel to Trishna's took less than 10 minutes and cost about 200 rupee, about $5 US. Since I had organized the group, I paid for the tuk-tuk, and Mary and Paula offered to pay the return fare.

Trishna's Restaurant was more formal than I'd expected. We were seated at an elegantly laid table with a linen tablecloth and napkins and china and silver. The host, staff, and servers were all uniformed. In casual dress, I felt somewhat out of place. I ordered chicken curry, naan, and jasmine rice, along with strong hot tea. Generous portions overflowed on several plates, and I certainly relished every bite! Paula enjoyed her chicken tikka while we all chatted about flying to India.

The server took my payment, but he quickly returned, setting some of my money on the table and quietly telling me it was not Indian money. Apparently I had accidentally mixed in Thailand baat with my Indian rupees. I apologized and promptly settled the bill with appropriate funds. Looking closely at the bills the server had returned, I saw they were clearly marked "Bank of Thailand"! Handling multiple currencies is one of the many challenges of regular international travel. Stuffed but happy, we survived the return tuk-tuk trip, arriving at the hotel shortly after 4:00 pm on that beautiful sunny Mumbai afternoon. Back in my room, I turned on the television and then took a shower. I nodded off for a post-lunch nap, sleeping soundly until my alarm clock awakened me at 9:00 pm.

~ ~ ~

Ladi and Fola Sheyabu were not leaving Mumbai until Saturday night, but they knew business obligations would keep them busy until the last minute. On Wednesday, November 26, a busy day for the Sheyabus, final negotiations for India's major purchase of Nigerian crude oil concluded at 5:00 pm, and they planned to celebrate that night. Fola hurried to the spa to get her nails done, while Ladi made a final visit to the shopping arcade's tailor to pick up two custom-made business suits. As he strolled through the shopping arcade, Ladi stopped at the bookstore to purchase a book for each of his three children - Clarise, Benjamin, and Adam. Ladi wanted to expose his children to different cultures and opportunities, so he carefully selected traditional Indian stories. After reconnecting at 6:30 pm, Ladi and Fola went to the hotel's bar to enjoy cocktails before their 8:00 pm dinner reservations.

~ ~ ~

Regina and two other GIA crew members ate at the Hotel's Indian restaurant and then went to the shopping arcade. Regina wanted to buy an Indian carpet for her 45th birthday on March 1, 2009. She had been looking for months on every trip to Mumbai, but she still wasn't able to find just the right one. She was exhausted. Perhaps next time ...

Katrin and Nina took full advantage of the hotel's luxurious outdoor pool. Warm water under the tropical sun, along with poolside drinks with little paper umbrellas...what more could a girl want at the end of November! Just 25 years old, Nina bubbled to Katrin about her fiancé Joachim, a police officer one year her senior whom she had met through her cousin. They had become engaged just two months earlier and were planning their wedding. Smiling at her enthusiasm, Katrin was genuinely happy for Nina. Sighing, Katrin told Nina that she had been married for five years. "We were school sweethearts," she said. "We were only 20 when we married, and that was just too young. We split up when I was 25 and had been with German International for only two years. Fritz simply couldn't cope with me flying and being gone so much. Be sure Joachim understands your work and your schedule." "Oh, he does," Nina assured her. "He's already come with me for a long layover in New York, and he wants to travel with me to more places." "Good," responded Katrin," just so long as he knows what he's getting into!" Chuckling about men, the two women left the pool area to get some sandwiches in the lobby for dinner and then headed to their 18th floor rooms for some sleep before their late night flight.

~ ~ ~

Mary, Paula, and Nicolas also napped in the early Mumbai evening. Tony and Juan took a tuk-tuk to Leopold Cafe at 5:00 pm and returned to the hotel at 7:00 pm to take a short nap. Ian fell asleep while watching ESPN in his hotel room.

Sam visited with his wife and children via Skype as they prepared for Thanksgiving without him. While Sam was disappointed at missing Thanksgiving with his family, he was holding December 25 through January 1 as time off. He was overjoyed at the prospect of spending the holidays at home. Jet lag kept him from sleeping. He wasn't looking forward to the long red-eye flight to Amsterdam even though he'd have a two-hour crew break along the way.

~ ~ ~

While my crew members, other than Sam, were napping, Samantha, Anne, and Debra were struggling through their Amsterdam-to-Mumbai flight. They faced challenges similar to those my crew had faced; passengers milled about the cabin while Anne and Debra conducted the duty-free service. With the holidays rapidly approaching, Samantha made a shopping list during the flight. She wanted to buy her mother and sister leather wallets and purses, and she hoped she could find matching items. Around 10:00 pm Mumbai time, Samantha, Anne, and Debra began their cabin service of pizza and soft drinks in anticipation of an 11:30 pm arrival in Mumbai.

~ ~ ~

Our crew was scheduled to be picked up at 10:50 pm, and we were to gather in the lobby by about 10:40 pm.

My nap ended when my alarm clock buzzed at 9:00 pm. I shaved and dressed while watching National Geographic television—a program called "Air Crash Investigation"! My hotel wake-up call was on time at 9:50 pm.

Fola and Ladi Sheyabu left the hotel restaurant, returning to their room on the 16th floor across from the elevators and down the hall from my room.

Regina, Katrin, Nina, and the rest of their crew were sound asleep in anticipation of their midnight wake-up calls.

Ian and Sam were just awakening from their naps.

Captain Daniel was sound asleep, waiting for a hotel wake-up call at 9:45 pm.

Nicolas was repacking his bags.

Paula stepped into the shower at 9:00 pm.

Mary was ironing her uniform.

Colleen had finished her room-service pasta dinner and placed the tray on the floor in the hall.

David woke up from his nap at 9:30 pm.

Tony and Juan arrived back at the hotel shortly before 9:00 pm after their dinner at Leopold Cafe. They hurried to shave and prepare for our late flight.

I wrote a postcard to Tiffany, my niece in suburban Detroit, planning to leave it at the front desk to be mailed. Tiffany always asked for postcards from anywhere interesting, and this would be her first from India. At 10:25 pm I walked down the quiet hall to the elevator bank on the 16th floor.

After receiving her wake-up call, Mary pulled her hair into its usual ponytail and gave it a quick spray. Her slightly unwieldy luggage was stuffed with her purchases, and she piled them together on her roller-board suitcase. Slipping into her high-heeled uniform shoes, she left her room a few minutes early to have coffee in the lobby before our pick-up.

Standing in front of the bathroom mirror, Colleen put the finishing touches on her make-up. The hotel was quiet, but above her she could hear the occasional muffled sounds of some sort of party taking place in a ballroom. She was glad the noise hadn't begun while she was sleeping. She thought some sort of night club must be gathering steam for the evening. As she packed her make-up, the noise escalated into a serious commotion with thundering steps, a muffled cracking sound...and screams. Concerned, Colleen stepped into the hallway outside her room.

Fola set out the suit she planned to wear in the morning and then brushed her teeth next to her husband. She slipped into bed with the BBC news quietly playing on the TV. Ladi turned off the bathroom light and slid into bed beside her. Using the remote, he turned off the television and wrapped an arm around his wife. Snuggling together, they fell into a contented sleep.

When the elevator door opened in front of Mary, she automatically stepped forward. But in the same instant, her brain registered something odd, so she blocked the door with her hand and looked inside. Blood. Bullets. Splattered blood. Gasping, Mary recoiled in horror and jumped a step back into the hall. As Mary caught her breath, the elevator door quietly closed. Mary instinctively turned to run.

Captain Daniel awoke with a start, realizing he'd slept through his 9:50 pm wake-up call. There was no voicemail from the hotel staff. Feeling uneasy, he picked up the phone and called the front desk. No one answered, and he knew something was very wrong. The hotel staff was far too professional to forget a crew member's wake-up call and then fail to answer a call to the front desk. Quickly pulling on jeans, t-shirt, and sandals, he rushed to the elevators, planning to go downstairs and find out what was going on.

David arrived in the lobby around 10:30 pm and made his way to the 24-hour lobby café. "A coffee, please," he said to the young woman behind the counter. A sudden, violent noise erupted at the hotel's front entrance behind him. He turned to see the tall man in the turban, the one who smilingly called tuk-tuk cabs for us, fall in a hail of bullets. The woman at the counter dropped the coffee. Frozen in shock, David instinctively clenched his fists.

As Ian finished in the bathroom, he heard Sam next door open his door and step into the hall. Hurrying to catch Sam before he walked down the hall, Ian opened his door and stuck out his head. "Hey, Sam, if you can hold on for a second, I'll walk with you." "Okay," Sam agreed, stepping over to Ian's door while Ian gathered his luggage. "Did you get any sleep?" Ian asked. "Barely!" Sam replied, yawning.

Finished styling her hair, Paula replaced the room's hair dryer and walked into the main part of the room. She paused, thinking she had heard something outside the hotel. It sounded like the staccato sound of gunfire. She looked out the windows, but the scene looked normal. A loud knocking on her door startled her, and she heard Mary crying out, "Paula! Open up! Let me in! PAULA!!" Rushing to the door, Paula wondered what was going on.

Tony pushed the button for the elevator and waited...and waited. After a few moments, he realized the elevator was taking too long to arrive. Pushing the call button again, he wondered what could be the problem. The hall around the elevator was quiet and peaceful, giving no clue that something very bad was happening in the hotel.

Nicolas tied his necktie and checked his look in the mirror. Hearing staccato bang-bang noises outside, he dismissed it as a car backfiring. When he heard it again and again in quick succession, he knew it was gunfire. Wondering what was going on, he looked out the window at Marine Drive below.

Juan packed his uniform vest into his luggage along with his necktie; it was hot and humid outside and on the crew bus, so he wanted to stay cool until on board the plane. He rolled his luggage down the hall to the elevators on the 18th floor.

I stood in front of the elevators on the 16th floor and pushed the call button. I didn't notice that the button didn't illuminate. I pushed the button again, and now I noticed it hadn't lit up. The elevator didn't come, and I began to grow annoyed. *It's close to pick-up time; I have to get downstairs,* I thought. Behind me on an attractive table was a house phone that automatically rang the front desk. I picked it up, but no one answered. *How strange*, I thought. Irritated, I returned to my room to call the front desk from my room phone. I figured that if the guest elevators weren't working, they could send someone up on a service elevator and escort me downstairs that way. Again, the phone went unanswered. *Maybe a flight cancelled, and the front desk is swamped trying to accommodate everyone*, I considered, trying to make sense of the situation. I still had to get downstairs, though. Finally, I pushed the phone's emergency number that autodialed the front desk. "WHAT?? Still no answer? What's going on??" I fumed. All sorts of bizarre ideas ran through my mind, trying to come up with a reasonable explanation for the silence. M*aybe something happened, and the hotel was evacuated as I slept,* was one of my thoughts. Returning to the elevators, I pushed the call button, hoping the elevator would come this time.

Paula opened the door. Before she could speak, Mary pushed her way inside. "The elevator's full of blood! When the doors opened, I saw blood splattered everywhere!" Mary said, physically shaking. "What happened?" asked Paula, expecting some explanation. "I don't know," answered Mary, "but something is VERY wrong. I was afraid someone was coming after me!"

~ ~ ~

The first explosion sounded at about 10:35 pm; it could be heard throughout the hotel. There was no longer any doubt that something VERY bad was going on.

~ ~ ~

"WHOA!" exclaimed Colleen, instinctively flinching.

Fola and Ladi sat up in bed. "What was that??" they asked each other in unison.

Juan felt the concussion ascend the elevator shaft, pushing a gust of air. He instinctively stepped back.

Paula and Mary froze in surprise and fear.

Ian and Sam made eye contact and wordlessly hurried into Ian's room.

Captain Daniel had been in the elevator heading to the lobby. When the doors opened at the lobby level, he saw a horrific sight. Devastation. Blood. Death. His brain could barely absorb it. Gunfire rang out, and he watched a man fall dead. Desperately pushing the "door close" button in the elevator and repeatedly punching his room floor, Captain Daniel could only think about getting back upstairs to his room. The elevator doors opened on his floor seconds before the elevators shut down. He was sprinting down the hall to his room when he heard, and felt, the explosion. "What about the rest of the crew?" he agonized as he threw open the door to his room and tumbled in.

Regina woke up; she wondered what had happened and tried unsuccessfully to call the front desk. Katrin jumped up from bed, threw on jeans and a shirt, grabbed her purse with her passport inside, and rushed into the hall. Nina pulled on sweat pants and a shirt, slipped into her sneakers, and hurried to the door of her room.

Just as Katrin rushed out of her room, Nicolas opened his door and saw Juan a few steps down the hall. Katrin ran to the rooms of the other GIA flight crew; she pounded on their doors and shouted in German. Seeing Nicolas and Juan, she added in English," It's a terrorist attack!"

~ ~ ~

The explosion occurred the second I pushed the elevator button; it almost felt as if I'd caused it. The concussion was startling. I felt the floor sway and the blast rush up the elevator shaft. The gust was so strong, the pressure made my ears pop. Fear welled up inside me.

Looking down the hall, my thoughts raced. The hallway was so still and quiet that I actually thought I might be alone in the hotel.

A door opened across the hall from me, and Fola Sheyabu looked out. Her hair in a wrap, wearing sweats and eyeglasses, Fola spoke to me in perfect English, "Do you know what's going on?" Sighing in relief that other people were indeed still in the hotel, I said, "That was a bomb. We'd better get out of here!"

In the lobby, David watched in horror as the terrorists cold-heartedly shot everyone in their path. He jumped behind the café counter, and the woman pushed him through a door into a back room. "Come!" she commanded and ran for a back service entrance. David followed, hoping they would escape the nightmare.

Sam and Ian looked out in the hallway as people began coming out of their rooms. A housekeeper came out of an adjacent room, set her cleanser bottle on her cart, and—gesturing toward the far end of the hall—told Sam and Ian, "Let's go this way." Sam called for the others in the hallway to follow. The housekeeper, Sam, Ian, and six other hotel guests entered a service elevator and descended to the mezzanine level.

Fola went back into her room and, a moment later, Ladi, also wearing sweats, stepped out. His demeanor was determined and stern, as if he was thinking "Who's instructing my wife??" We made eye contact, and I said, "Hello." "Hello," he replied in perfect English. Sizing me up, he realized I was relatively calm and wearing a flight attendant uniform. He visibly relaxed, probably deciding I wasn't a weirdo of some sort. "Do you think it's serious?" he asked. "Yes, I do," I replied. "We need to get out of here. The bomb could have started a fire." Ladi nodded, "Yes, that's true." I was more frightened than I let on, and I could feel the tension in my body. While Fola was in their room gathering their passports and wallets, Ladi and I heard a breathless panicked voice over a speaker in the hallway, "We've had an incident in the hotel! Stay in your room! We will let you know when you can leave your room!" I looked at Ladi and said, "I don't believe that! Whoever said that is in a state of complete panic. We need to get out of here now." "Come inside our room for a moment," Ladi invited me. He propped open the door as we entered. "I tried calling downstairs," I told them. "May I try again from your room phone?" "Yes, of course," replied Ladi. "I'm going to call my office and see if they know anything," said Fola dialing her mobile phone. "No answer from the front desk," I sighed, hanging up the phone. "Let's get out of here now." Fola said, "OK, I'll call you later," and she ended the call.

As we exited their room, another guest met us at the open door. "Sorry. Do you know what's going on?" asked Heidi Low of Alpine International Airlines. "We're evacuating. Come with us," I said. "May I leave my luggage here for now?" I asked Ladi. "Of course," he responded. The four of us walked toward the stairwell next to the elevators. Heidi reached the door first, pushed it open, and began hurrying down the stairs. I was next, followed by Ladi and Fola. The stairwell was quiet and well lit. We had descended about two floors when Heidi turned a corner, stopped abruptly, pressed her hand to her mouth, and gasped in horror. I immediately noticed her eyes slightly glaze over in shock. Stepping next to her, I glanced in the direction she was staring. The full extent of our problem was immediately apparent. There was blood splattered on the landing and walls. Bullet shells were scattered on the floor, along with a blood-soaked cloth. I immediately realized that so much blood meant death, and death meant the attack on the hotel, more than a simple bombing, was ongoing. I knew we couldn't continue down the stairs as terrorists were probably nearby. Turning to Ladi and Fola, I hollered, "We can't go this way! There's blood everywhere!" Ladi stopped and turned to look back at Fola, whose face registered a mask of horror. "Go back! Go back!" I shouted, my adrenaline pumping. Fola and Ladi quickly turned around, rushing back up the stairs to the 16th floor. Grabbing Heidi by her left hand, I barked "Come on!" and pulled her up the stairs with me.

~ ~ ~

Looking into the hallway from Paula's room, Mary and Paula saw Colleen across the hall at her door also staring into the hallway. "We'd better get out of here," Colleen announced. "We have no way of knowing whether or not the hotel is on fire." "Yes," agreed Mary, "let's get out of here." "Bring your flashlights, keys, wallet, and crew identification cards," directed Colleen, closing her room door and carrying her tote bag into the hall. Mary also had her tote bag, but Paula just carried her purse. All three women were in uniform, wearing matching navy short-sleeved dresses, pantyhose, and black pumps. Despite Mumbai's heat and humidity, Paula and Colleen also wore uniform red button-down long-sleeved sweaters. "Where are the others?" Mary asked. "We should try to find the rest of the crew." "Let's stop at the floors as we go down and see if we can find anyone," suggested Paula, as they began to descend the same stairwell my group had just attempted.

Nicolas stood at his open door watching other members of Katrin's crew enter the hall following Katrin's alarm. Juan hurried over and said, "I'll go down and see what's going on. Stay here until I come back." "Alright," responded Nicolas. "I'll see if there's anything on the television about this." Leaving his door open, Nicolas turned on the local TV news. At the moment, though, nothing was being reported about the attack on the hotel.

Regina told the seven other GIA crew members gathered around her in the hallway, "Stay together. We don't yet know what's going on." Using her mobile phone, Regina texted her husband Lutz in Frankfurt, telling him that an attack was happening at the hotel but that, at the moment, they were safe. A captain at GIA, Lutz called GIA's employee emergency number and provided the first sketchy information about the attack. Regina quickly texted each flight attendant's name to Lutz. "I'm sure this isn't too serious," Regina assured the crew, "but stay together." Nina was terrified, her eyes reflecting her panic. Her arms were pulled tightly in front of her, and her thumbs were pressed to her lips. Despite Katrin's attempts to console her, Nina was frozen with fear. *I'll have to keep her—and everyone—calm*, thought Regina. "Why do I get the hysterical ones?" Regina texted to her husband with a small inner chuckle.

Juan descended the stairs toward the lobby level, but he stopped at the mezzanine level when he heard shouting and crying below him. "The lobby's been destroyed," a woman sobbed, "and I saw bodies!" The hair on the back of Juan's neck stood up, and he shivered involuntarily despite the warm air. He turned and rushed back up the stairs to tell Nicolas what he'd heard.

Ian, Sam, the six other hotel guests, and the housekeeper leading them reached the mezzanine level and joined a large group of people gathering in a large conference room. The dining tables had been pushed aside to accommodate the crowd. As other guests and employees continued to arrive, Ian and Sam anxiously searched for other TIA crew members, but none arrived. "Where are they??" Sam lamented. "I hope they're alright," Ian replied automatically although he was unsure about his own well-being at the moment.

The force of the explosion still ringing in his ears, Tony frantically fumbled through his uniform pockets for his room key before realizing that he'd left it in his room. *I can't get back into my room*, he thought in fear and swallowed his tears. Stepping into the hallway from their rooms were a tall blond man, Paul Bjornmark from Sweden, on Tony's left and an Indian man, Umesh Parwari, on his right. Terrified, Tony looked back and forth between them. "What happened?" asked the Indian man. "A bomb!!" Tony choked out. The men gathered together as the hall speakers came to life with the panicked voice telling guests of the "incident" and to remain in their rooms. "I left my key in my room," Tony blurted. "Come to my room," said Paul. "May I come with you?" asked Umesh, "I'd rather be with people until we know what's happening." "Of course," Paul responded, "Let's stay together." The three men rushed to Paul's room down the hall.

Captain Daniel slammed shut his room door, attaching the security bar. Knowing that wouldn't stop an all-out attack, he pulled the room's desk in front of the door, shoving it into the small alcove between the room and the door itself. Then he grabbed the phone, relieved to hear a dial tone. He quickly pulled from his wallet his pilot's emergency checklist card and direct-dialed TIA's Systems Operations headquarters in Minneapolis. After one ring came the recorded greeting telling him "Welcome to the System Operations Center. To report an emergency, please press…" *Dear God*, he prayed, *please help the rest of the crew. Where are they?* While the cheerful elevator music played in his ear, he grew more and more exasperated as he waited for a human to pick up his call.

In the mezzanine conference room Sam, Ian, and approximately 50 other hotel guests and employees waited for instructions. Although Sam and Ian didn't know how or why they had been guided to this room, the hotel employees seemed to have a system of some sort. Hotel security officers arrived and directed everyone to an emergency exit on the street side of the room. The double doors opened to a short staircase leading down to the sidewalk below.

David ran through the kitchen and into the back delivery halls behind the lobby, following the woman from the coffee counter who was leading a group to the hotel's back delivery entrance. Gunfire continued in the lobby, and the screams and shattering glass echoed through the space, ringing in David's ears. Suddenly an explosion in the lobby overwhelmed them. The blast force literally lifted David up, knocking him and the others off their feet. Kitchen items crashed to the floor. Falling hard and certain he was about to die, David prayed aloud, "God, please let my wife know how much I love her."

We rushed back into Ladi and Fola's room, leaving the door open. "What was it?" Ladi asked, now visibly anxious. Fola wrapped her arms around herself, looking at me with palpable fear. Heidi, obviously traumatized by the sight of the blood in the stairwell, stood beside me. I stammered, "There was blood everywhere! People must have been killed! This is worse than I thought." "What should we do?" Fola asked fearfully. "I don't know…let's try to find another exit," I said, looking out into the hallway for other guests.

When the women arrived on the 16th floor, Paula shouted for me. Forgetting my name in the confusion, she called "Don!" just as I was looking out in the hallway. "Over here!" I called. "We have to go! Come on!" exclaimed Colleen. "We can't use those stairs," I replied, "This is bad. People have been killed." "Let's try the other stairs," suggested Heidi. "Let me put my luggage back in my own room for when we come back," I said as I rushed toward Room 1609. "Bring your flashlight, passport, and crew ID," reminded Colleen. I grabbed the items out of my tote bag, turned to go, and then remembered my keys. Taking them, I rushed back to the others in the hall. Another woman came out from her room, sleepily asking, "What's going on?" "A bombing. We're evacuating. Come with us," I answered. As a group, Heidi, Ladi, Fola, Colleen, Paula, Mary, the sleepy woman, and I started down the second emergency staircase.

Someone Sam guessed to be a manager opened the emergency door, instructing everyone to exit the building. Ian and Sam made their way to the sidewalk, which was in complete chaos. Police cars with flashing lights were everywhere; army trucks were arriving; soldiers in full combat gear were pouring out by the hundreds; the street was being cordoned off by barricades; people were being ordered away. "My God," Sam said in disbelief, "This is huge! The whole city is under attack!" Before Ian could respond, the Indian soldiers began shouting commands in Hindi. "What??" stammered Ian in confusion. A hotel employee translated the commands into English for the bewildered foreigners. "Run! Quickly! RUN!" Sam and Ian followed the others, running for their lives.

David leapt to his feet, running with the others amid the panic and confusion toward the rear service doors. As he reached the rear hall, one door was already open, and people were pouring out into the delivery area behind the hotel. Shaking from exertion, shock, and adrenaline, David stepped into the warm night air, into a scene of utter chaos. Police officers arrived, shouting commands in Hindi. The crowd, about 25 in total, began running for the sidewalk at the end of the loading dock. David followed blindly, not knowing where he was headed. *Just get me the hell out of here*, was his only thought.

Tony, Paul, and Umesh rushed into Paul's room. "We're under attack!" exclaimed Tony. "I'll call downstairs, or try to call my fellow crew members." He dialed "O" for the hotel operator, but the phone rang and rang, unanswered. Umesh tried to use his mobile phone, but the circuits were busy. "What should we do?" asked Paul, of no one in particular. "Let's barricade the door until we know what's happening," suggested Tony. "When it's safe to leave, the hotel should call us." Together the three men piled an end table and a chair in front of the door. Tony suddenly realized that, with the phone working, he could call TIA. "I'm going to call my company," he told Paul, "and I'll make sure you don't have to pay for the international call." He picked up the phone and direct-dialed TIA's Detroit Inflight Office.

Our group had descended to about the 11th floor when we met Juan. He was climbing up from the mezzanine level, out of breath and visibly shaken. Holding up his hands in a "stop" gesture, he gasped, "No, no, you can't go down. The lobby's destroyed." Colleen very pointedly asked, "Then what do you think we should do?" "I left Nicolas upstairs. He's waiting for me in his room on the 18th floor," responded Juan. Resigned, we turned around and followed Juan up the stairs.

"The hotel's been bombed," Regina texted to her husband. "We're waiting together with a crew from America." Lutz texted back to tell her he would call GIA's management to tell them something was up. "Good," Regina responded. "We might not make the flight tonight." Nina was fidgeting in fear, and her eyes were glazed over and distant. Regina didn't like the way Nina looked, and she hoped the situation would be resolved before Nina lost control. Katrin stayed close by Nina, instinctively knowing that Nina needed to be watched and protected. Tension began giving way to despair as they waited, glancing into Nicolas's room to see him and the television.

Finally, Captain Daniel's call to TIA was answered, and his heart skipped a beat. On the other side of the world, TIA's systems operation center duty desk manager Candice Price recited her usual spiel, "Name and employee number?" "Daniel Abbott! Employee number 797191! I'm in Mumbai, India, and the hotel's under attack!" "What?" stuttered

Candice, not really comprehending the situation. "Get the director on the line!" barked Captain Daniel commandingly. "This is an emergency!" "You have an emergency?" Candice questioned. "One moment." "NO!! Don't put me on hold!" blurted Captain Daniel. But he was too late, and Candice's voice was replaced by elevator music.

The police had cordoned off the street and, as Ian and Sam ran blindly, they saw the first military transport truck arrive, the rear tailgate open, and dozens of soldiers getting out. Gasping for breath as their group neared the end of the block, Ian saw a solitary uniformed policeman, flanked by other men in plain clothes that he guessed were also police officers. The uniformed officer was gesturing at the opening to an alley, and the others were waving their arms in a "come this way" gesture. "Sam," hollered Ian, "over there!" Ian, Sam, and their group were the first to arrive in the police-secured holding area for hotel evacuees.

David and the others with him were running a short distance behind another group of evacuees. David saw the police officer gesturing toward an alley and, adrenaline pumping, he ran for the alley. A hotel chef, clutching his tall white hat in front of him, was first to run into the alley trailed by other kitchen staff. Next around the corner was David, followed by at least four front desk staff dressed in long saris that hadn't slowed down their progress at all. Confusion reigned in the alley, with people calling out for others as more groups poured in from the hotel. David, in his uniform, was easy to spot, and he heard, "HEY! You're one of the flight attendants!" Sam and Ian rushed up to him, grabbing him by the hand. "We're the pilots," Sam said. "Are you alright?" Barely able to speak, David slumped against the alley wall his eyes ill focused and shock beginning to register in his demeanor. "Yeah, I'm OK," David absently responded. "Have you seen the others? Are they coming behind you?" Sam asked. "I don't know," stammered David, tears beginning to form in his eyes as the shock and horror threatened to overtake him. "They must be dead," he mumbled.

The alley in which the groups were gathering was about a city block from the hotel. Running beside a multi-story garage serving a vertical downtown galleria mall, the alley provided access between the garage entrance/exit and the street. The mall was closed for the night, and the police or military had accessed and secured the garage to use as a holding area for hotel and local evacuees. Sam, Ian, and David sat at the entrance to the second-floor access slope. Sam pulled out his phone and, when it found a satellite signal, he nearly wept with relief.

~ ~ ~

Inbound TIA Flight 36 from Amsterdam landed in Mumbai on schedule at 11:30 pm. Seated at the back of the plane, Samantha and Debra smiled in anticipation of a fun layover. "Make sure you have your bottle of water," Debra reminded Samantha. "I have it and a Pepsi for later!" As they waited for the passengers to deplane, they heard a two-tone chime that indicated a call to all flight attendants. The women picked up their phones, identifying themselves by door number and location. "Door four left." "Door four right." Their flight captain Marvin Ross was on the line. "Stay on the plane," he told them. "There's been some kind of attack downtown. I'm not sure if we'll be going to the Trident-Oberoi or not. When I know what's going on, I'll let you know."

Not understanding the depth of the crisis, Debra sighed with irritation and said, "Something always happens on my flights; if it's not one delay, it's another!" Looking out the window, Samantha said, "Hopefully this won't take too long. But I'll bet now there won't be time for drinks in the crew lounge if we want to get up early to shop." The women pulled their luggage up the aisle to the business class seats to gather with the rest of the crew.

~ ~ ~

In Minneapolis, the director of corporate security, Richard Santini, was not having a good day. There was a developing "semi-crisis," in Thailand: a coup d'état had disrupted airline operations there, and a TIA crew was probably going to be stuck for two or three days until the airport resumed full operations. Candice suddenly burst into the room and demanded he take a call from a pilot having a major delay in Mumbai. "What could be so important?" he sighed, taking the call from

Captain Daniel. "Hello, this is Richard Santini. I understand you're having a delay in Mumbai?" he questioned. "We're under attack! This is Captain Daniel Abbott. I'm in Mumbai, and we're under attack!" Richard looked sharply at Candice then calmly said "OK, Daniel, tell me what's happening."

~ ~ ~

Our group trudged up the stairs, exiting on the 18th floor. Regina, Katrin, Nina, and their group were huddled outside of Nicolas's room. Most appeared composed, although I could see that Nina was on the edge of hysteria. Ladi, Fola, Juan, Paula, Mary, Colleen, and Heidi crowded into Nicolas's room. I stopped to speak to Regina's group, speaking softly and calmly. "Is everyone alright?" Katrin looked at me and nodded, unshed tears shimmering in her eyes. "Come inside with us," I said. "I think it's better for all of us to be together."

I was concerned about Nina. She clung to Katrin, afraid to be alone. Her eyes were unfocused, and her expression registered barely contained panic. I could see she was barely holding herself together. I hated seeing Nina, and the others, so afraid. These first signs of unadulterated terror changed the situation for me, and I resolved to project calm confidence and some sense of normalcy. We all turned to the television for news. We were a random group of multinationals brought together by misery and circumstances beyond our control, seeking safety, strength, and support in each other's company.

~ ~ ~

Gathered in Flight 36's business class, Debra and Samantha waited for information along with the other crew members. Captain Marvin and the station manager, Raj Kansupada, hurried back down the jet bridge from the airport's departure gate. Anne, who was dozing in a seat, awoke to the sound of heavy footsteps in the jet bridge. "We've got a problem," Captain Marvin announced. "There's a full-fledged terrorist attack going on downtown. The Trident-Oberoi Hotel was bombed, and the city is under military blockade. This is really bad, so we probably won't be staying here. TIA is going to have us refueled, and we'll probably fly out to Dubai. We don't know how long this airport will stay open, so we might have to leave here quickly."

Samantha's heart skipped a beat. "Terrorist attack? The hotel's been bombed? What??" Her thoughts raced. Debra exhaled out loudly, as if she'd been punched, and slumped into a seat. Anne was the first to speak. "What about the crew in the hotel?" "I don't know," responded Captain Marvin, "but it doesn't look good." "I called the transportation company," interjected Raj, "and they said the crew never made it to the pick-up." In the silence that followed, Samantha felt nausea well up inside her. "I'm going back to the phone," said Captain Marvin, "I want to find out what they're going to have us do." He and Raj went back up the jet bridge. Tears began rolling down Debra's cheeks. Although she wanted to comfort her friend, the nausea took over and Samantha rushed into the nearest lavatory, the crew's stunned silence ringing in her ears.

~ ~ ~

Candice, at TIA's System Operations in Minneapolis, answered her second call in five minutes with her standard greeting and heard, "Hello! Hello! This is first officer Sam Wilson, employee number 243800! We're in Mumbai, India, and we're under terrorist attack!" A bit confused, Candice said, "You're in Mumbai? Is this Daniel Abbott again??" "NO!" cried Sam, "I'm the first officer working with him. Mumbai's under attack, and we're in a garage." "OK; you're also in the attack. Let me get Mr. Santini." "Don't put me on hold!!!" Sam thundered. "I won't; just hang on," responded Candice. "Richard!!" she called out. "We have more crew on the line in Mumbai, outside in a garage." Richard was still talking with Daniel in the hotel, and he interrupted Daniel and said, "Other crew are alive; they're outside in a garage." Richard didn't want to put Daniel on hold, and Candice was talking with Sam on the other line. Richard turned toward the assistant director seated in an adjacent office and hollered, "Jim! We need you here on the phone right now!"

Sam, Ian, and David sat huddled together on the concrete garage floor as bombs sounded in the distance and gunfire echoed down the street. Sweat beaded on Sam's forehead in the tropical Mumbai heat. David's skin began to take on an ashen pallor, and his eyes were glazed over in shock. Sam knew he'd never forget the look on David's face. Ian was quiet. None of them spoke the words they were all thinking: Were they the only crew survivors? What happened to the rest of the crew? Chaos reigned around them, as hotel guests and employees milled around, stunned and shocked at the life-or-death situation in which they found themselves.

Jim Snodgrass took the phone from Candice and said, "Sam Wilson? This is Assistant Security Director Jim Snodgrass. Where are you? Are you alright?" "Mumbai is under attack. Three of us escaped from the hotel: me, second officer Ian Reid, and flight attendant David Johnson. We're in a garage secured by police and military. We don't know what's happened to the rest of our crew. Oh, my God, oh, God." "Stay on the line with me; can you do that?" Jim asked, looking to Richard for guidance. Realizing this was definitely a full-blown crisis, Richard instructed Candice, "Call a Code Red, Candice. Full crisis; full crisis."

~ ~ ~

Samantha, still feeling queasy but with her nausea under control, splashed water on her face and rinsed out the sink, then found a bottle of water in the galley and rinsed out her mouth. Debra, now more composed, was deeply afraid of the clear threat to their safety. Samantha and Debra speculated on the other crew's status ("Maybe the crew was picked up and the transport company is wrong; maybe everyone was able to leave the hotel before the attack.") as well as their own potential danger ("What's going to happen to us? Where will we go? The airport must be a big target; will we be attacked?"). Although the tension grew, several flight attendants slept from pure exhaustion. Tears in her eyes, holding Samantha's hand, Debra softly cried, "I want to go home. I just want to go home."

~ ~ ~

Fola sat at the desk chair in Nicolas's room, and Ladi stood beside her. Regina, Nina, Katrin, and their group stood near the door, with Mary, Paula, and Colleen next to them. Nicolas sat on the bed, Heidi leaned against the wall outside the bathroom, Juan and I stood beside the window looking out at the deceptively quiet street below. Sketchy news reports began filtering in. Gunfire had been reported both in the Taj Mahal Hotel and in our hotel, the Trident-Oberoi. The main train station had been attacked. Gunfire was reported in the streets of the downtown financial sector. But there was nothing to indicate what we should do or where we should go.

Upon hearing outside gunfire, Paula told me to close the curtains so we wouldn't be seen. I just closed the sheer curtains, thinking they'd obstruct us from outside view but I'd still be able to see the street. "No," Paula said, "that's not enough. They can probably see in here. Close the heavy drapes, too." I closed the drapes and turned back toward the room, in time to see Katrin look up from her mobile phone. The look on her face, unforgettable, is burned into my memory. "The news says the hotel is on fire," she cried, tears running down her cheeks. Nina screamed, her arms wrapped around herself. Regina looked up from her phone, and I faced them across the bed. For a millisecond, no one spoke.

~ ~ ~

At TIA, a "Code Red" meant only one thing: a MAJOR incident or accident had occurred. It could mean an airplane hijacking, an emergency evacuation, or an airplane crash. It also meant the immediate notification of key personnel including the pilot and flight attendant unions; the chief pilot and the flight attendant's base manager; the director of TIA's disaster response team; the director of TIA's corporate security; the director of sales who was included in case an emergency call-in center had to be activated; and others.

~ ~ ~

Midnight in Mumbai was 1:30 pm in Minneapolis on Wednesday, November 26, the day before Thanksgiving. Margaret Olsen, TIA's

Disaster response team director, put the finishing touches on an email
to her counterpart at another airline and hit send. At that moment, her
office phone rang, while the emergency ring sounded urgently on her
company cell phone. She knew instinctively that this was not a drill.
Grabbing both phones, Margaret heard the pre-recorded emergency
message on her cell phone at the same time she heard Candice exclaim
on the office line, "Code Red, Margaret. Code Red! Get over to
Operations NOW!" Margaret pulled her response manual out of her
desk drawer, grabbed her cell phone, which was still playing the
recorded emergency announcement, and ran upstairs to the Systems
Operations Center.

Captain Daniel blurted out all he knew, and Richard scribbled it down.
Sam and Jim did the same. Sam's immediate worry was the status of
his cell phone battery. While he wanted to stay in communication with
Jim in Minneapolis, if his cell phone battery died, they'd lose the
connection. Together, they decided texting might use less battery
power, so Jim sent Sam a text from his personal cell phone. Initially
terrified to end the call with Richard, they decided it was best for
Captain Daniel to call Minneapolis at regular intervals. They were
concerned that a ringing phone in his room might draw attention to
Daniel. Having piled the mattress and box spring, along with an
upholstered chair, into the small vestibule with the desk to barricade
the door, Captain Daniel dragged the bedding into a corner of the room
away from the door, set the phone beside him, and prayed.

~ ~ ~

After receiving the first text from Jim, Sam turned to Ian and David and
said, "Pray for the others. I hope they're alive somewhere." David
remained silent, and Ian cleared his throat and looked at the floor. Off
in the distance, staccato gunfire continued to echo.

~ ~ ~

Mumbai had been brought to its knees that night. Pakistani extremists
had struck at the heart of India's financial capital. The city's two main
"western" hotels were under siege. In a volley of gunfire, hotel

employees and guests fell dead. The initial attack in the Trident-Oberoi felt like it lasted a lifetime, with machine gun fire blasting throughout the elegant marble-floored lobby, but it lasted only moments. The restaurant became a scene of death and chaos, where moments before guests had been relaxing over Indian and western cuisine. Elegantly dressed diners dove under tables, ran for exits, or threw themselves over loved ones in the hope of protecting them. Furniture was overturned. Dishes and glassware shattered. Bullets ricocheted off the marble floor, embedding themselves in the walls, piercing the safety glass windows, and riddling the paneled walls. In those first few chaotic minutes, approximately 10 hotel employees and 20 hotel guests died, with many more injured.

The Taj Mahal Hotel fared no better. Mina Sherafudin, a newly hired 21-year-old front desk receptionist, was speaking on a hotel telephone with a guest on the 11th floor when bullets began flying. With a cry, Mina dove to the floor, screaming into the phone, "Stay in your room!" Dropping the phone, she half-crawled and half-ran behind the wall into the back office. Then she and two other women crowded into a broom closet, the only available hiding place. Listening to the screams and death cries echoing from the lobby, Mina shook, feeling suddenly cold, and her teeth chattered. The three women huddled on the floor, clutching hands, and prayed.

~ ~ ~

The terrorist attack caught the Mumbai police force by surprise, and the police call center was swamped with urgent reports. Along with the hotels, the train station, and Leopold Cafe, a hospital and a Jewish community center were part of the attack. With the full extent of the attack unknown, the Indian Army was called in to help, and police immediately began cordoning off streets and ordering people to evacuate the area, hoping to minimize the risk to civilians. With any luck, they'd be able to confine and apprehend the terrorists. Confusion reigned in Mumbai, and much remained unknown at midnight on Thursday, November 27.

~ ~ ~

In response to Nina's scream, Colleen emphatically commanded, "Stay calm!" "OK," I said, addressing the group, "we have to go." I gestured toward the door. "How many are we?" I asked no one in particular. Counting 18 of us, I said, "Stay together!" We all filed out of the room and into the familiar stairwell. Regina clutched her phone, Colleen lugged her tote bag, and I carried my computer bag. We hurried, but we weren't in a panicked rush. Barbara, one of the GIA crew, struggled to keep pace with the rest of us as we descended. I kept chanting to myself, "Get to the lowest possible floor! Get out of the building! Keep everyone together. We'll all get out of here." Along the way, Juan said, "We can't go all the way to the lobby since it's been bombed. Let's stop a floor up and see if we can find another exit." That was a good idea, and about five or ten minutes after we left Nicolas's room, we reached the mezzanine level and stepped into a deserted hall. The time was about 12:30 am.

~ ~ ~

Having barricaded the door to Paul's room, Tony, Paul, and Umesh wondered what to do next. Umesh called his wife in Delhi on his cell phone, as soon as circuits permitted, learning from her the extent of the attack. Wisely, and emphatically, she instructed him not to leave the room under any circumstance and to be quiet, since the terrorists were searching the rooms. Paul's computer was connected to the hotel's internet service, and he was able to Skype to his fiancée, Eva, in Stockholm. Upon hearing what was going on, Eva sobbed but quickly regained her composure and thought through the problem. She decided to call the emergency number for the Swedish diplomatic corps; maybe they would know what to do. Telling each other "I love you" before hanging up, Eva promised to Skype back to him the moment she had information. Taking stock of the situation, Tony realized it was about 1:30 pm in Detroit. He held his breath while he waited for the phone to ring halfway across the world.

~ ~ ~

Still on board the plane at Mumbai International Airport, Samantha, Debra, and Anne huddled with the rest of the crew of Flight 36. "I was supposed to be on the crew that was at the Trident-Oberoi. Paula and Mary wanted to fly together, so I traded with Mary," Anne said slowly. Feeling they ought to leave the plane because it might be a target, Anne then suggested, "Maybe we should go into the airport and watch the news on a television." "NO!" exclaimed Captain Marvin. "No one is leaving the plane. We might have to take off in a hurry, and I won't risk anyone wandering off." Suddenly, Samantha thought of her sister, Teresa, an executive with Global Airlines in Washington, D.C. If she could contact Teresa, Samantha thought, she might know something or be able to help somehow. Walking onto the jet bridge with her cell phone, Samantha nearly wept with relief when it connected to the airport's wireless Internet. She rapidly texted, "Teresa! I'm in Mumbai! There's a terrorist attack going on; do you know anything?"

~ ~ ~

The well-lit mezzanine level hallway in which my group found itself appeared to be completely cut off from the other hotel corridors. Locked doors closed off at least two conference rooms. Ladi and Juan rushed to the glass doors leading to the outdoor pool, but the doors were locked. Under ordinary circumstances, the view of the pool, illuminated by bright outdoor lights, was stunning; tonight, none of us even noticed. We only saw the locked door preventing our escape. Standing beside me, Monika of GIA said to no one in particular, "I'm trembling inside." With a brave smile of reassurance, I patted her on the shoulder and said, "We're alright now. The worst has passed." She smiled back, humoring me by appreciating the gesture but understanding we were far from safe. Regina looked around; Nina clung to Katrin; Colleen clutched her tote bag.

"Let's break a window," I suggested. "We can find something to use; maybe a piece of furniture." "NO!" said Regina. In unison, she and Nicolas then said, "They'd hear us." "We have to get out of sight,"

Nicolas continued. *Where*? I wondered. We had no access to anywhere else from our location, and all the doors off the hallway were locked. On impulse, Mary tried the double doors of a conference room and discovered that, rather than being locked, the doors were simply tied shut with a cloth from the inside. As she pulled the doors as far open as they'd go, Mary knocked and called, "Hello? Hello? Is anyone inside? We're unarmed hotel guests." There was no answer, so I pulled out my small pocket-sized flashlight, shining it through the crack between the slightly open doors. All we could see was a table set with glassware and the curtain behind the table. "I don't think there's anyone in there," I said, pulling on the doors in an attempt to loosen or tear the cloth holding them shut. "I can't get the door open," I sighed in frustration. "Let me use this!" exclaimed Paula, fumbling for a tiny box-cutter on her key ring that she used to cut security bands sealing the duty-free carts on board the airplane. "YES!" I cheered, pulling the doors open as far as I could. Paula tried to cut the cloth, but her hands were too big to fit in the small opening. Handing the cutter to Nina, Paula said, "Here. You try it." Although she was shaking, Nina was able to cut the cloth. The doors swung open, and I shined my flashlight inside. We clicked the light switch, illuminating a well-set private dining room or small conference room, and we all stepped inside.

~ ~ ~

"Whatever you do, stay in your room!" Richard instructed Captain Daniel sternly, again on the phone from Minneapolis. "Don't answer the door! Don't answer the phone! Don't draw any attention to yourself!" "What about the rest of the crew?" asked Captain Daniel miserably. "Have you heard anything at all?" Taking a breath, Richard cautiously responded, "We have Sam on another line. He, Ian, and at least one flight attendant are out of the hotel in a garage area set up by the police." "Out of the building?? How did they get out?" Captain Daniel was thrilled but shocked. "I don't know yet, but they did," replied Richard. "And the others?" asked Captain Daniel. "I wish I knew...but I don't," said Richard solemnly. "But you can't let anyone know you're in your room. We heard that the terrorists are searching room to room." "I'll sign into Skype," suggested Captain Daniel. "Can you join Skype from the office?" "We will," said Richard. "Meantime, keep this line free, unless you're calling here." Turning to Candice, Richard ordered, "Get us on Skype, NOW!"

~ ~ ~

Raj ran down the jet bridge to the crew still aboard inbound Flight 36, his footfall echoing in the tinny space. Captain Marvin met him at the airplane door. Rushing up to the Captain and out of breath, Raj blurted out, "I have the crew list for the outbound crew!" Taking a deep breath he thrust the list at Captain Marvin. Stepping into the plane towards the crew, Captain Marvin quickly perused it. Reluctantly, Samantha looked over Captain Marvin's shoulder as he read the list out loud, "Nicolas Dumont purser, Colleen Ballard, Paula Burns, Mary McAlister, Juan Lopez, Douglas O'Keeffe, Tony Park, and David Johnson. Captain Daniel Abbott, first officers Sam Wilson and Ian Reid." Samantha wrapped her arm around Debra as Debra choked out, "No. Oh, no, no, no! Doug's on the list! He's a friend of mine." "Tony Park," mumbled Samantha, feeling the nausea churn her insides again. "I know Tony; we've flown together so many times..." Her words trailed off. Everyone fell silent, trying to absorb the knowledge that people they personally knew were caught up in a terrifying disaster happening at that moment. They couldn't reach them; they couldn't help them; they couldn't do anything. Captain Marvin asked Raj if Minneapolis had word about their departure. "I've been on the phone with TIA," Raj continued, "No word yet on your departure, but TIA is still trying to get you clearance to leave. At least you're done refueling, so you can depart the moment you're cleared." Debra was sure the attack would reach them in a matter of time. They were on a fully fueled US aircraft with a big American flag on its tail, a big target for any terrorist group. Debra silently begged God for help.

~ ~ ~

The day before Thanksgiving in the US is always a busy travel day. Wednesday, November 26, 2008, was no exception. In TIA's inflight offices it was business as usual for a busy day. Crew members arrived from and departed for their trip sequences; front desk staff managed the office phones; and flight attendant managers addressed the routine demands involved in managing the volume of personnel based at Detroit. Only the Systems Operations Department was aware of the situation being faced by their crews in Mumbai. In fact, they had quietly deleted the Mumbai trip sequence from the computer; only someone viewing the Mumbai sequence on their computer would have noticed the deletion. Deleting the crew list was meant to secret the crew names from circulation and the inevitable spread of misinformation. Unfortunately, the crew lists exist in numerous locations so complete confidentiality was impossible. As our whereabouts were unknown, TIA struggled to keep our names secret until they knew our circumstances.

A few minutes after 1:30 pm, TIA's main switchboard phone rang. Front desk manager Shauna McNally answered it with her standard "Detroit Inflight, this is Shauna." "Hello! Hello!" said a voice breathlessly. "This is flight attendant Tony Park, employee number 007143. I'm in India! We're under attack!" "What??" Shauna said, startled. "Tony who?" "Tony Park. Please! I need to speak to a manager. Mumbai is under attack!" "What's your employee number, again, Tony?" Shauna asked, typing it into her computer as Tony repeated it. Checking the system, Shauna told Tony, "The outbound flight has been cancelled. Stay on with me." Leaning over to a second computer terminal, she brought up an Internet search engine and typed in "Mumbai." Her heart sank when she saw the news of the attack. "Tony," she asked calmly, "Where are you?" "I'm in Mumbai," he said with exasperation. "I mean, are you at the hotel?" "Yes! I'm in a room with two other people. We're under attack!" Shauna signaled another staff member and said, "Get me the Director! Now!" To Tony, Shauna said, "Tony, you're on the room phone, right?" "Yes." What's the number on the phone? What's the number of the room you're in?" Tony told her, while Shauna set up a three-way call so the Detroit base director could join her and Tony.

~ ~ ~

Samantha heard her cell phone chime indicating her sister Teresa had answered her text. Wiping away her tears, she rushed towards the boarding door where the airport wireless connection was stronger. She was relieved as the text opened, but what she read quickly erased her feeling of relief. "You're in a war zone!" Teresa texted, "Can you get out of there?" "No, we're still on the plane at the gate," Samantha responded, quickly adding, "Don't tell mom. I don't want her upset." Samantha looked forlornly at the airport, which appeared to be operating as usual. Planes taxied by, ground operations continued, and people walked through the terminal. Everything seemed normal at the airport, but downtown was in chaos. "How can this be happening?" Samantha wondered aloud, as if someone would hear and provide an answer.

~ ~ ~

We entered and looked around the room. It was about 30 feet long by 12 feet wide. Wood paneled, with built-in shelves at one end, the room's entire exterior glass wall looked out on the outdoor pool and the beautiful gardens beyond. Floor-to-ceiling tan drapes ran the length of the window wall, and beige carpet covered the floor. In the center was a long table surrounded by a dozen chairs and set with elegant glassware, empty water pitchers, pencils, notepads, and dishes filled with hard candy. Four buffet tables were draped in floor-length white tablecloths: two were to the right of the door through which we had entered and the others were in front of the windows. At the other end of the room was a door, locked with a deadbolt, which opened to a different part of the hallway, which was shaped like a U surrounding the room on three sides. Occupying the corner near that door were two wing-backed chairs with an end table between them. There was, unfortunately, neither a telephone in the room nor a television we could have referenced.

My mind struggled to make sense of the situation. I thought we were overreacting, that it wasn't—simply couldn't be—as serious as some were making it out to be. I thought, *We'll just sit it out here around the table until we're able to leave the building*. The knowledge that our lives were in danger stayed below my consciousness because I refused to see that reality. Looking at my companions, seeing the terror in their eyes and the worried expressions on their faces, I hated that they were so frightened. I remained calm...blissfully ignoring the underlying menace surrounding us. My friend, Joanne, later said my behavior reminded her of a quote, "If you can keep your head while all around you are losing theirs, it's quite possible you haven't grasped the situation!"

As we settled into the room, Fola sat, elbows on the table, with her hands over her face, barely containing the tears shining in her eyes. She just wanted to get out of the hotel. I walked over to her and silently patted her shoulder, not wanting to intrude. Paula and Mary sat down in the wing-backed chairs. Regina, Katrin, Nina, Monika, and the GIA group sat along the wall. Lifting up its tablecloth, Heidi and Colleen squeezed under a buffet table, ready to pull the tablecloth back down if the need arose. Juan joined Fola at the table, while Nicolas, tense and restless, paced around the room. Ladi stood near the door with his arms crossed, anxiety radiating from him. Suddenly, and seemingly out of nowhere, a hotel employee arrived at the door and stepped into the room.

~ ~ ~

Downtown Mumbai was in complete chaos, with the police force overwhelmed and disorganized. Martial law was declared when the Indian military was called in to assist. The soldiers were in charge of dealing with the terrorists. Downtown Mumbai was closed to pedestrian and vehicular traffic. Armed guards surrounded the evacuees in the garage off the alley near the hotel. Those of us remaining in the hotel knew nothing of what was going on outside. We only knew the hotel was under attack, we wanted to get out of the building, and we wanted to stay alive.

~ ~ ~

At TIA's Detroit base, Shauna told director Nancy Sullivan that she had a flight attendant on the phone with an emergency, adding Nancy to her call with Tony. When Nancy picked up her phone, the first thing she heard was Tony crying out, "They're trying to kill us!" Seeing that the Mumbai sequence had been deleted from the computer system and listening to Tony's panic, Nancy knew the situation was very, very bad. "Tony, do you know what's happened to the other crew members?" she asked. "No. They're probably dead," Tony responded forlornly. Nancy's heart sank, and she told Tony, "I'm going to call Minneapolis. Stay by your phone so we can call you back." "OK," agreed Tony, clutching his phone and wondering what to do next.

~ ~ ~

Hoping to see the rest of the crew, David, Ian, and Sam scanned each new arrival at the entrance to the alley/garage. David's face was ashen. His phone had no signal in Mumbai, so he couldn't call his wife Shannon although he really didn't want to upset her anyway while he was still in danger. Gunfire echoed in the distance, and David flinched. He stood and stretched, walking to the opposite side of the alley to look at the crowd. "David!" called Sam, "Stay with us! I need to know where you are!" Gloomily, David returned, sitting on the concrete floor next to Ian. "David, we're in a war zone," Sam explained, "We might be the only members of our crew to get out of here alive. Please don't tempt fate by walking around." David nodded his acquiescence. Around them hotel guests, employees, and soldiers milled about in the warm Mumbai night.

After Sam had given Jim in Minneapolis the most vital information about the terrorist attack, he hung up. About every 15 minutes Jim or Richard would text Sam, checking on him and exchanging any new information. Sam repeatedly asked, though afraid of what he might hear, about the rest of the crew. "We don't know," Richard texted in reply. While he'd heard from Captain Daniel, the captain's safety was not yet completely assured, so he didn't mention it to Sam. "There's been no word yet from any of the other flight attendants," Richard said. Sam looked at David and Ian afraid to share that information.

~ ~ ~

Standing on the jet bridge texting with her sister, Samantha learned more about what was happening in Mumbai than anyone had been able to provide to the crew aboard Flight 36. Mumbai was a war zone, Teresa texted. Scores of people were feared dead and hundreds were likely injured. The city's main international hotels, including the Trident-Oberoi, had been bombed, were on fire, and were under siege. The main train station had been destroyed. "Samantha, whatever you do, stay at the airport!" Teresa ordered. Samantha quietly returned to the plane and sat down. Her mind was flooded with possible scenarios, all terrible. The attack had decimated downtown Mumbai, and surely the airport was a target...how long would it take the terrorists to reach the airport? Samantha decided to keep the news to herself at the moment. Her decision to do so hung upon her concern the new information could have upon Debra as well as upon the rest of the group if they felt even more imperiled.

~ ~ ~

As a precaution, Nancy Sullivan in Detroit and Richard in Minneapolis, decided to also conceal the crew information for Flight 36. While they knew the flight was—at that moment—safe at the airport, the crew was in a war zone, and anything could happen. *No sense worrying families*, thought Nancy, making a quick decision that the crew's emergency contacts would be told that the flight was held in Amsterdam and that the crew was safe—if they were told anything at all. It was a relief to know that Tony was alive; the question was how to get him out of the hotel. Richard told her that a plan was under consideration to hire commandos who would extricate Tony and Captain Daniel. "This is more serious than I realized," Nancy sighed, picking up the phone to call Tony back.

~ ~ ~

Flight attendants throughout TIA's extensive route system began to spread news reports of the attack. Those familiar with the Mumbai sequence quickly calculated the time difference and realized that the crew was probably in the hotel when the attack began. Despite TIA's attempt to keep the names of the crew members confidential, resourceful flight attendants were able to obtain crew lists. Those lists weren't all 100% accurate, but, absent sick calls or trip sequence trades, the lists were close enough. Cell phones began to ring.

My former roommate and ex-boyfriend, Russell, was on a layover in Seattle when he got a call from his friend Ken, who had a copy of the crew list from my flight. "Have you heard from Doug?" asked Ken. Being unaware of the attack, Russell said, "No. Is something up?" "There's been a major terrorist attack in Mumbai. Doug's listed as part of a flight crew that might have been in the hotel when it was attacked. Do you know if he kept the trip?" "He would have," responded Russell, beginning to worry. "He loves those Amsterdam layovers! Is the crew alright?" "We don't know," said Ken, "but this is bad. I won't be surprised to learn they've been hurt...or killed. Can you call him?" "Yes, and I'll e-mail him, too," said Russell. "Let me know if you hear anything. I hope he's OK," Ken said. "Me, too," responded Russell. "I'll turn on CNN news to see what they say." Ending the call, Russell turned on the hotel room's television and saw the screen fill with terrifying images from Mumbai. His apprehension growing, Russell dialed my cell phone, but his call went to voicemail. *Not a good sign*, he thought. He quickly sent an e-mail to me, hoping for the best.

~ ~ ~

Shocked to see our group gathered in the room, the hotel employee looked at Nicolas and asked, "What are you doing here??!" He didn't identify himself, and none of us had seen him before. I moved closer to Nicolas to listen. "Why are you here?" he demanded. "We came from upstairs," said Nicolas. "We're trying to get out of the hotel, but the doors are locked." "OK. Terrorists are still in the hotel, and they're looking for people to kill," the man told us. "Stay in here. Don't leave this room! Turn off the lights and bar the door. We'll try to get you out." Hearing that, Ladi took Fola by the arm, leading her to the far corner of the room. He sat beside her, putting himself between her and the door, prepared to cover her with his body. Colleen was still curled up under the buffet table, and Regina squeezed into a small space between Ladi and the buffet table. Nicolas turned off the lights. Katrin and Heike pulled the unused buffet tables in front of the door in an attempt to barricade it. Then Katrin, with Nina beside her, sat on the floor along the wall. I turned on my small flashlight and walked over to Mary and Paula, who were sitting in the wing-back chairs. "Turn that light off!" hollered Katrin, and I complied. My eyes began to adjust to the dim light coming under the doors from the hallway and the outdoor lighting coming through the curtains along the glass wall.

We'll just wait here, I thought. *This isn't so bad. We'll wait here until we can leave.* But the room was filled with dread. We were trapped in the dark. We couldn't leave the hotel. We couldn't fight back against the unseen enemy. I felt bad for having pulled Ladi and Fola out of the safety of their room; perhaps if they'd stayed upstairs, they'd be alright. Sadly, I accepted the situation, but I still wasn't really afraid. The others were.

~ ~ ~

Concerned that terrorists might be calling individual rooms, Captain Daniel and Richard devised a phone signal. Richard told Daniel that he was not to answer the phone; he was to let the call go to voicemail then call Richard back. Tony, Paul, and Umesh decided that when their phone rang, Umesh would answer it. If terrorists were calling the rooms to see who was hiding, they thought that an Indian man's voice answering the phone wouldn't arouse the same suspicion as a foreign voice. Their TIA contacts in Minneapolis gave strict orders to both Captain Daniel and Tony not to leave their rooms unless fire put their lives in immediate danger. The men had no idea how long they'd have to stay holed up, but they all understood that being barricaded in their rooms was the safest possible place for them to be.

~ ~ ~

Margaret Olsen, TIA's Disaster response team director, skidded into the Systems Operations Center in Minneapolis, clutching her emergency manual in her left arm and stuffing her cell phone into the right-hand pocket of her slacks. Her breath caught at the sight of the beehive of activity and the numerous people on the phones. This was big. Very big. Jim quickly briefed her, "Margaret, we have a full-blown terrorist attack in Mumbai, India. Two crews are caught up in it. One crew, on inbound Flight 36, is still on the plane at the airport in Mumbai. The outbound crew for Flight 35 was in the hotel at the time of the attack. The three pilots are alive, and so are at least two flight attendants. But we have nothing on the other six flight attendants. We know the captain and one flight attendant are trapped in their hotel rooms; the other two pilots and another flight attendant are outside in a secured garage area. Mumbai is under martial law, and the attack is ongoing."

Televisions and computer screens displayed grisly images of death and destruction. Margaret saw the Taj Mahal Hotel on fire. "Show me the crew list," she requested. "Who are the ones we know are alive?" Studying the crew list, the attack hit home, becoming personal when she saw my name. Margaret had trained me as a "Family Assistant Volunteer" to respond to the needs of air accident victims or their family members. She gulped as she saw that I was listed as "missing."

Richard and Margaret had decided not to notify the family members of my crew until they had concrete information about those of us considered missing. The risk of spreading inaccurate information was simply too great. But the news was already spreading. On Flight 36, Samantha's sister Teresa knew where Samantha was. "Do you want me to have Teresa call your family?" Samantha asked Debra. "Yes, please," answered Debra, wiping away her tears. Modern technology circumvented even the most carefully laid disaster response plans.

~ ~ ~

Huddled in the dark room, everyone was jittery. Every little noise caused us to flinch. The room was thick with anxiety and tension. Regina was on her cell phone with her husband in Frankfurt. "We're hiding," she whispered. "There are about 15 or 20 of us, and we're barricaded in a conference room on the mezzanine level. About six or seven are from another airline's crew; I think they're Americans. I'm going to ask them for their airline's emergency number. Tell GIA Operations where we are!" "Ja," he agreed, sweat breaking out on his forehead and his breath catching in his throat. "Stay out of sight, Regina. And let's switch to texting to keep your phone quiet. I love you, Schatz (treasure)." "I love you, too," Regina said, ending the call.

Nicolas looked around, counting the TIA crew members: himself, Juan, Paula, Mary, and me. "Where's Colleen?" he asked. "I'm under here," Colleen miserably answered from under one of the buffet tables. "Are you alright?" Nicolas queried. Colleen didn't answer. Hurrying over to the far side of the room, where Paula, Mary, and I were, Nicolas said "You guys, I think it's better if you come over with the rest of us rather than spreading out around the room." "OK," answered Mary vaguely. "Do you know where Tony and David are, or the pilots?" Paula asked. "I have no idea," Nicolas answered, and then I contributed, "I don't know where they were in the hotel. Hopefully they're safe." Looking stern, Paula took Mary by the hand and we all walked across the room to join the others.

Colleen wrapped herself into a ball, hugged her knees, and prayed, "Thank you, God, my daughter's not here. Please help us." Tears rolled down her cheeks. Katrin was so tense her shoulders hurt. Heike began texting with her husband in Frankfurt, her face illuminated in relief by the light of her cell phone, "In case I don't make it out of here, I love you, Schmoozy," she texted. Fola was quiet, fearing that speech would cause her to lose her composure and knowing this was no time for hysteria. On his phone, Ladi accessed Indian news. What he saw made his stomach flip. "HOSTAGES BEING TAKEN AND KILLED IN THE HOTELS," screamed the headline. "Foreign nationals targets for murder." Quietly he tucked his phone back into his pocket and looked at Fola. He didn't want to say anything to her, or anyone else, for fear that a deadly panic would sweep through the room. So Ladi said nothing and simply prayed for help.

As she sat on the floor with her back to the curtain-covered windows, Paula thought back to her early flight attendant training. In the case of a hijacking, pre-9/11, flight crews had been instructed to blend into the crowd, if possible. Removing her crew member wings and name bar from her uniform dress, she dropped them into her purse and instructed all of us to remove our crew identification. Even though I thought it a bit ridiculous because it wasn't a hijacking situation, I dutifully removed my necktie and my blazer with all its crew pins, then rolled them up and stuffed them into my computer bag. Suddenly, from out in the hall, we heard footsteps...and we all froze.

~ ~ ~

Tony, Paul, and Umesh sat quietly on the floor, listening to the far-off gunfire and footsteps. Voices echoed in the hallway, and Tony shuddered in fear.

Captain Daniel sat on the floor in his nest, made with blankets and sheets; his mattress was part of the barricade at the room's door. The room phone rang, startling him, but he didn't pick it up until he saw the voice mail message light blinking. After verifying the voicemail was from Minneapolis, he prepared to return the call. Suddenly, he heard gunfire down the hall, and he hung up for fear his voice would be audible to the gunmen. He reached for his computer and sent an email to Richard in Minneapolis, "Gunfire in the hall; can't be on the phone right now."

~ ~ ~

On Wednesday, November 26, my Amsterdam friend Ronald and his partner sat down to dinner. Ronald glanced at the television in the background. The evening news reported, "Terrorist attack in Mumbai. Scores killed or injured. Overwhelmed police have been joined by the Indian army, and martial law has been declared." Ronald didn't think much of it. *Mumbai is a big city*, he thought. *There's not much chance that Doug was involved.* As the cold, rainy Dutch night wound down, Ronald returned to his dinner.

~ ~ ~

Based in New York City, my flight attendant friends Mari Asai and Marilyn Luker prepared to greet passengers boarding their flight from New York to Minneapolis and on to Portland, Oregon. They had been shaken to see my name on the pirated Mumbai crew list, and they hoped I was alright. At Marilyn's suggestion, she and her fellow crew members had a moment of silence for the crew in Mumbai and then returned to their work as passengers began walking down the jet bridge.

~ ~ ~

We listened in frozen silence to the footsteps passing by in the hallway. Holding her breath to stop crying, Nina clutched Katrin's hands. When the footsteps passed by our room without stopping, we began to take grateful breaths. I was sitting on the floor in front of Ladi and Fola and next to Nicolas and Juan; my eyes had adjusted to the dim light. I kept repeating to myself, "This is an airline layover; this can't be happening; we're overreacting." Time seemed to stop, and I had no idea how long we'd been in the room. I began to get concerned about the lack of a restroom, wondering what we all would do if we had to hide much longer. Lying on the floor, Barbara and Monika closed their eyes and tried to relax. We kept movement to a minimum and our voices quiet. Tension ebbed and flowed in the room.

Regina, knowing we were very definitely NOT safe, found the strength to act. Between texts with her husband she scrambled out of her corner to our TIA crew group. She asked me, "What's your airline emergency number?" I just looked at her, my mind unclear, and words failing me. I thought, *Oh, how sweet. She's trying to help.* When I didn't respond, Regina turned to the others. "What is your emergency number? I'll call it and have my husband call, too. He's a captain at GIA. One of our airlines can surely help us!" "Try Scheduling," said Juan, whispering the Scheduling number from memory. Regina dialed it then swore, "Verdammit! It's not working. Is there another number?" She texted the Scheduling number to Lutz, hoping the number would work from Germany. "How about Inflight?" offered Mary. "YES! Try Inflight," I said, as Mary gave the number to Regina. *Get yourself together*, I commanded myself, realizing that a passive panic state would be deadly. Suddenly, Katrin whispered loudly, "SHHH! Quiet!" We froze, listening to more footsteps in the hallway.

~ ~ ~

Aboard Flight 36 an exhausted Samantha returned to Debra. "It's bad, Deb," sighed Samantha in resignation. "I'm going to try to get some sleep," responded Debra. "I hope we'll be able to leave soon." Debra and Samantha stretched out and tried to relax in their business class seats. Around them, the rest of the crew also tried to nap. Tears running slowly down her cheeks, Samantha prayed, "Dear God, please protect the crew in the hotel. I beg you, dear God, I beg you."

~ ~ ~

Random groups of traumatized, breathless evacuees continued to sporadically arrive at the safety of the secured garage. Watching the alley entrance from the second floor, a GIA captain would ask if anyone from GIA had arrived, and Sam would inquire about TIA crew members. The GIA crew members were thrilled as a few more of their group arrived. Sam, Ian, and David, though, remained the only TIA crew members in the garage. "Pray for the others," Sam said. Each group of traumatized survivors that arrived only caused disappointment for Ian as no TIA crew were among them.

~ ~ ~

Time stood still for an eternity until the footsteps passed. Fola let out her breath, Nina relaxed her grip on Katrin's hands, and Colleen cried quietly. I rose to my hands and knees and then sat down on the floor. The tension was becoming unbearable. I began to seriously wonder what would happen if we didn't get out of the room sometime soon.

~ ~ ~

At the Mumbai airport, it was as if nothing had happened in Mumbai. Planes landed and took off; passengers and crews bustled about. Aboard Flight 36, Debra managed to fall asleep next to Anne, and

Samantha, too, napped between texts with her sister. Station manager Raj called everyone he could to obtain information. Initial reports from friends downtown were discouraging; waiting for conclusive information, Raj said nothing to the Flight 36 crew. He was certain, though, that in all likelihood the missing TIA crew members were dead, since they had not contacted Minneapolis or made it to the safety of the garage. The night wore on.

~ ~ ~

Tony, Paul, and Umesh continued to get information in and out by phone; with his local accent, Umesh was designed to answer the phone whenever it rang. Barricaded in the safety of his room, Captain Daniel resolved to speak with Tony as soon as he felt he safely could.

~ ~ ~

All of Mumbai shook from the attack. Police and the Indian army swarmed through downtown Mumbai. They secured the train station and began dealing with the dead.

~ ~ ~

In the Taj Mahal Hotel, barricaded in a closet with other employees, Mina phoned her parents. "The hotel's under attack. I love you. I'm calling to say goodbye," she softly cried.

~ ~ ~

In Minneapolis, Richard, Jim, and Margaret tried to account for each member of Flight 35's crew. They were depressed and frightened as they worried about the welfare of the six missing members of the crew. Unaware that we were hiding in a conference room, they prayed for our safety.

~ ~ ~

The Trident-Oberoi's memorial to the attack

Doug next to the Trident-Oberoi's memorial to the attack

Doug in the conference room of the Trident-Oberoi

A view of the conference room as it appeared during Doug's visit in 2012

Nina was overcome with fear, primordial fear. Would she be hurt? Tortured? Killed? Raped? Would she watch other people being killed? How long would she be confined in this room? Would she ever return home? Would she ever again see Joachim, her fiancé? Her nerves were shot. She simply couldn't take freezing in terror every time she heard footsteps outside the room. All she wanted was a cigarette. Yes, a cigarette. Yes, that would calm her nerves, she decided. It would OK to have just one.

Once the footsteps passed and she released Katrin's hands, Nina slowly picked up her purse. In the dim light, I saw Nina's silhouette as she stood up. I could tell by the faraway look in her eye that she was not clear-headed. Crossing the room to the corner near the wing-back chairs, Nina sat at the far end of the table. Then I watched in horror as, in slow motion, Nina reached into her purse, took out a cigarette, placed it between her lips, flicked her lighter, and lit it.

"UGH!" groaned Ladi. "Somebody's smoking?!?!" asked Juan in disbelief. "SHIT!" swore Mary. Regina looked around, trying to see the culprit. I saw the amber glow of the cigarette and instantly smelled the smoke. "Put it OUT!" Nicolas urgently blurted. I joined the fray, saying, "Put it out! You'll get us killed!" "Put it out NOW!" barked Ladi. "Oh, God, no!" cried Paula, "Now they'll know we're here!" Katrin jumped up, fearing that the erupting commotion in the room could get everyone killed for sure—and Katrin did NOT want to die. In a few quick steps, Katrin was at Nina's side. She snatched the cigarette from Nina's mouth, extinguishing it in a dish. Nina finally lost her composure and began to get hysterical. Quickly, with determination and compassion, Katrin wrapped her arms around the young girl. Speaking in German, Katrin whispered to her, "Nina, honey, you simply cannot smoke now. We absolutely have to stay hidden; we can't do anything to alert the terrorists to our position. Come back to the group and stay with me. I won't leave you alone, I promise." Like a robot, Nina, now softly, uncontrollably, started crying, stood up, and permitted Katrin to lead her by the hand back to the group. Katrin looked at the rest of us and said, "She's gone a bit crazy, but she'll be OK now." Katrin sat on the floor; Nina curled into a fetal position, crying, with her head on Katrin's lap. Katrin soothingly stroked Nina's hair.

I felt so sorry for Nina, and I wished I could have done something to help. Having shut off my own fear in order to cope with the situation, I felt infinite compassion for the others and their terror. I was particularly affected by the awful, dead expression in Nina's eyes. Colleen crawled out from under the table to sit beside me on the floor. I turned to her and smiled reassuringly. Outside, we could hear the attack rage on.

The hotel employee who'd discovered us alerted the police and the army now in the hotel. Additionally, GIA alerted its station manager at the airport that crew members were hiding in the hotel, thanks to Regina's call to Lutz who alerted GIA's operations center to the trouble. The station manager also called the Mumbai police. Although we didn't know it, plans had been made to evacuate us from the building. The difficulty was how to accomplish this safely. Due to our location on the mezzanine level, there was only one logical route...through the devastated lobby. One group of soldiers positioned themselves in the lobby to protect our escape while a second group followed the employee to our conference room.

"We've been discovered!" I realized, turning from Colleen when I heard voices and footsteps in the hallway. Footsteps, heavy booted footsteps and a lot of them, stopped outside the door. Katrin and Nina froze, Nina sitting up and grabbing for Katrin's hands, not bothering to wipe the tears from her face. Fola silently prayed to God, over and over, "Save us; save us all, dear God." Clutching Fola's hand, Ladi made sure he was between his wife and the door, shielding her as much as possible from whomever was on the other side. Regina texted Lutz, "Someone's here!!" Then she curled into a ball, tucking her head between her knees. Paula, clutching Mary's hands, was certain she was dead, we were all dead. "Please God," she prayed, "make it quick so we don't suffer." Paula closed her eyes, waiting for oblivion to claim her. Under a buffet table with Barbara and Heike, Monika pulled the tablecloth tightly shut, hiding them from view. Colleen slunk to the floor on her stomach beside me, holding her hands beside her face so she could cover her eyes when the shooting began.

Still in denial, I sat facing the door thinking this couldn't be happening on a simple airline layover. Katrin, looking over our group, saw me sitting up, and quietly barked, "DOWN ON THE FLOOR!" Obeying, I hit the floor between Colleen and the door. I stared directly into Colleen's eyes, but she didn't even see me through her utter, inexorable terror. The look in her eyes reminded me of kaleidoscopes I'd seen as a child. *I'm glad she's behind me*, I thought. *When they shoot, my body might save her*. I felt the carpet scratch my cheek and saw booted feet through the crack at the bottom of the door. I heard Fola hold her breath, frozen in time. The room was shrouded in silence as we waited for the end to come, imagining what it would feel like to die.

~ ~ ~

The door cracked open about an inch, all the barricading would allow. Looking up from the dim light at floor level, I saw a white cloth squeezed through the crack, waving vigorously. "Hello! Hello!" said the welcoming voice of the hotel employee. "I know you're in there! GIA crew! It's OK; I'm the employee who found you earlier. You're safe! Unblock the door!"

We all began to breathe, relaxing with sighs of relief. Regina looked toward the door; Katrin loosened her grip on Nina's hands; Heidi crawled to the door and tentatively peeked through the crack. "It's OK!" repeated the hotel employee. "The army is here to get you out!" Katrin stood up to join Heidi, and the two women quickly began pushing the furniture aside. Nina remained cowered on the floor. Someone turned on the light switch, and the room was illuminated by bright lights.

With her eyes still closed, Paula thought, *Am I dead?* Sensing light in the room and hearing others stirring, she slowly opened her eyes. Seeing the activity at the door, Paula exclaimed, "Mary, come on!" I stood up and extended my hand to help Colleen to her feet. Still somewhat frozen by fear, Colleen rose next to me. Katrin took Nina by the hand, leading her to the door. In a burst of movement, Ladi hopped up and forcefully guided Fola through the door. Juan and Nicolas jumped up to join Paula and Mary. None of us spoke as we all filed out into the hall, blinking in the light.

Along with the hotel employee, there were about eight Indian soldiers in full battle fatigues lining the hallway, holding automatic weapons that looked as big as they were. The last to leave the room, I stared at the soldiers, registering surprise at their height: No soldier stood taller than my shoulder, and I'm 5'11"! But they certainly looked formidable. "Line up," instructed the employee. "Stay together. We'll take you downstairs and outside to safety."

As the soldiers began ushering the first of us down a flight of utility stairs, Heike suddenly ran back into the room. I turned to see what she was doing and had a bit of a chuckle as I saw her emerge with her purse! With my hand on her back, I guided Heike in front of me as we began descending the stairs behind the rest of our group. Soldiers were in front and behind us.

On the lower floor we entered the hotel's business center. The computers were on, and some of the monitors displayed web pages. *The Internet is still working; was the attack really so bad*? I wondered. We continued through another door into a hall landing that ran the full length of the indoor wall of the hotel's atrium lobby. A grand staircase descended to the palatial lobby in front of the main hall that led to the business office of the hotel, formal conference room, the gymnasium, and the spa.

At our first look at the lobby, we all froze, overwhelmed by the horror below us. Nina pressed her fists to her mouth. Colleen gasped, clutching her tote bag. Fola and Ladi turned away. Heidi, Barbara, and Monika clung to each other for strength. "Hurry!" implored the employee, "We must get out of here! RUN down the stairs, across the lobby to the hall." He pointed to the entrance to the shopping arcade, a straight line from the base of the stairs.

To get to the safety of the shopping arcade hallway, though, we had to pass through the lobby—the scene of destruction, devastation, and death.

The lobby. Overturned furniture. Blood and human debris spatter. Bullet holes. Smashed dishware. Shards of glass. Scattered papers. Pools of blood. Bodies. Once manicured potted plants were strewn about, dirt spilled out of shattered pots. Not a single window in the expansive atrium lobby remained intact. The safety glass had exploded into tiny gravel-like bits of glistening and shining glass that covered the stairs and the lobby floor like snow. Inexplicably the fountain in the center of the lobby continued to bubble away though awash with debris. Emergency lights illuminated the terrible space.

The soldiers with us gestured us to hurry down the stairs, while soldiers at the bottom of the staircase pointed urgently toward the shopping arcade hall. The women in their high-heeled shoes were frightened of slipping on the round pieces of safety glass, so they moved slower than the soldiers wanted.

The airline teaches us to bark evacuation commands in short, staccato bursts. The concept is for crew to act as drill sergeants in an emergency to get people moving away from harm. When I saw the women slow down at the base of the stairs, my training automatically kicked in and I shouted at them, "Come this way! Come this way!" I waved my right arm in a broad "come this way" motion. My words jolted Barbara into action, and she began running towards me followed by Monika. As I turned to continue running, I came up behind Mary struggling with her tote bag, her high heels skittering on the glass. "I've got it!" I gasped, grabbing her tote bag in my left hand and reaching for her with my right hand. Mary and I joined hands, running through the lobby wreckage towards the others in the shopping arcade hall.

We paused a moment in the shopping arcade, where the merchants' goods were exposed through the broken glass. Handbags, dresses, jewelry, and medicines were covered in the gravel glass, and I noticed that no one had looted the merchandise. Colleen and Nina were both still in the throes of blind terror, jumpy and panicked. Katrin, close by Nina, took a moment to peer through a blown-out window at the street in front of the hotel. Juan, realizing his shallow breathing would slow him down, commanded himself to catch his breath. I returned Mary's bag, thinking, *We're safe. We're out. They'll take us to a bus and get us to the airport.* Soldiers quickly ascertained safe passage for us through a blown out window.

Stepping through the window, the hotel employee cut through a flower bed onto the pavement of the portico. "Come! Come!" he ordered, "Outside NOW!" Without hesitation, Heidi hurried outside, followed by Katrin and Nina, Ladi and Fola, and the others. I was the last one through the window, expecting to be safe now that we were out of the hotel.

The streets outside the Trident-Oberoi Hotel, usually congested, noisy, and teeming with traffic, were silent. No traffic sped chaotically along the streets; no horns honked; no tuk-tuks spewed exhaust. No ordinary people, just police officers and soldiers. In the silence, Mumbai took on a surreal, post-apocalyptic appearance. The magnitude of the attack struck me once again.

On the portico, our group halted and lined up. I don't recall whether we were instructed to do so or instinctively did so. From my position at the end of the line, I could see the entire line of us in front of me. An Indian soldier ran to kneel behind me, with a machine-gun pointed back in the direction from which we had come. Other soldiers stood beside and in front of us. We weren't sure what to expect. Suddenly Mary shouted in terror, "Put your heads down!" to those in front and then behind her. Paula shuddered, thinking we were being lined up for execution. From my vantage point I watched all the heads in front of me duck down. Regina texted Lutz, "We're out! We made it!" From the front of the line, a soldier shouted something in Hindi; not understanding, we remained still. The employee translated, "RUN!" He repeated the instruction, accompanied by urgent gestures.

I took a step out of line towards him and pointedly asked "Run?" "Yes!" the man blurted with a hint of exasperation at our inaction "RUN!" Without hesitation I turned toward the others and shouted "RUN!" waving them forward with my hands as I took my first running step forward. Katrin shouted "LAUF!" in German and took off at full speed. Nina was in a panic, too frozen to follow Katrin until Regina took her arm and pulled her along. Colleen, struggling with her tote bag and her heels, tried to run. Nicolas tried to grab her tote bag, but she swatted him away, moving as fast as she could blind panic preventing her from realizing Nicolas was trying to help. We all ran for our lives.

But where were we going? I ran towards the Citibank branch office across the street from the hotel, adrenaline pumping through my body in a primal flight instinct. Katrin immediately arrived at my side. Safely across the street, I turned back to help the others, but a plain-clothed man waved me forward down the street and shouted, "NO! Keep running! Keep going!" I learned later he was one of the many off-duty police officers in plain clothes who had come to help. The man madly gestured to us, pointing toward more men about a block away. As we ran, I managed to glance back. I was relieved to see Fola and Ladi behind me, followed by Nicolas, Mary, Paula, Heidi, Colleen, Nina, Regina, Juan, and the rest. We all ran as fast as we could.

Far down the block, I could see several men standing on the otherwise deserted sidewalk, and I continued running toward them. Nearly side by side Katrin and I were the first to reach the men. "It's alright; you're safe here," said one of the men, ushering us into an alley. I recognized the alley as being next to the big multi-storied mall we'd visited earlier...was it only hours ago? It seemed like a lifetime had passed.

As many as one hundred people milled about the alley and in the adjoining garage: a man in a tall chef's hat, women in elegant dinner attire, uniformed hotel employees, and hotel guests in various stages of dress, including pajamas. Many different languages could be heard. People were milling about, some calling for companions and loved ones, some crouching in shock, others wandering aimlessly about the space. One man cried in Italian desperately searching out a travel companion. A pair of medics attended to those most in need.

To the left of the alley's entrance, I stopped to catch my breath. Colleen scampered into the alley in a terrible panic, shaking all over and her eyes still holding the "kaleidoscope" look I'd seen in the conference room. As the others arrived and joined the crowd, a male voice called down from the second floor. He was speaking German, and I recognized the words "German International Airlines." Thrilled, Katrin shouted back, "Yes! We're from GIA!" He told her to come up to the second floor. Sam heard the exchange and hollered, "Anyone from TIA?" "YES!!" whooped Nicolas, looking to see who had called out. "Come over here! How many of you are there?" asked Sam. Seeing Sam and Ian, I breathed my first real sigh of relief, knowing others of my crew had survived. As we headed to join them, I said to Ladi and Fola, "Come on, you're part of our crew now."

Standing by the stairs to the garage's second floor, Katrin waited for Regina, Nina, and Heidi and guided them upstairs. Regina took a deep, relieved breath, and then caught herself. "Where are the Americans? Katrin, did you see where they went? Where are they?" "They made it," Katrin assured her, "but I don't know where they went." "I have to go find them," Regina announced, turning to go back downstairs. "NO!" the GIA captain ordered, assuming full authority over the crew. "If they got out, they're alright. You can't go running around." "But...," protested Regina. "NO!" repeated the captain. "You have to stay here. That's an order!" Unhappy, but resigned to obeying the captain, Regina sat down on the concrete floor with a sigh. As Regina and her crew gathered on the garage's second floor, they joined numerous crew members from both the Frankfurt and Munich bases. Several French International crew members were also present. Heidi looked for other Alpine International crew members but found none. Shuddering to consider their fate, Heidi huddled with her German counterparts.

While Regina worried about us, I worried about our German companions. "Where are they?!" I cried out to the others. "I don't know where they went," Mary said. "They got out with us, so they must be here someplace." Determined, I told Sam, "I have to go find them. We need to stay with them; we've been through so much. It's better if the GIA and the TIA crews are together." "NO!" decreed Sam, in the same tone of command the GIA captain had used. "We just found you; you're not leaving us." Colleen sat on the concrete ramp; with her arms wrapped around her legs, she rested her head on her arms and wept, releasing her tension in tears.

The alley was in the shape of an "L," occupying one side and the back of the garage adjoining the mall. In the two places where the alley met a street, the openings were blocked off by soldiers and barricades. The soldiers were keeping the evacuees safe in a contained area, while ensuring the terrorists couldn't breach the barricades. We were on the concrete access ramp to the upper floors of the garage abutting the alley. To my right was a waist-high concrete wall that opened to the floor of the ramp above. Beyond the wall was the exit lane from the alley. Beyond the alley was a cluster of upscale multi-storied apartment buildings. I could see the flicker of television screens through the apartment windows. It seemed unreal that people were sitting in their homes, watching television while there was a terrorist attack happening on the street below!

"OK, everyone!" thundered Sam as if he was a drill sergeant and we were recruits. "Gather round. We're going to do a briefing. Sit down in a circle. Everyone, now!" I sat down heavily, motioning to Fola and Ladi to join the circle. Somewhere in the distance, I heard a faint explosion in the warm, clear night. Colleen unfolded herself, her tears still falling as she struggled without much success to regain composure. She sat to my left, with Fola and Ladi to her left. David sat to my right, his skin still ashen. Facing uphill, down the parking ramp and across the circle from me, were Juan, Mary, Paula, and Nicolas, their backs to the crowd. Sam and Ian sat between Ladi and Mary. Juan wiped his brow with a handkerchief and shook from the recent rush of adrenaline.

The street lights adequately illuminated the space, and we all looked around the circle at each other. Sam said, "OK, everybody. Thank God we're all still alive. I want a headcount of our crew, starting with me: ONE!" Around the circle we went, counting off. Nine out of the 11 crew members were present; we were missing Captain Daniel and Tony Park. Thinking of the two of them, we all grew painfully quiet. Continuing to maintain his authority and keeping us focused, Sam asked, "Does anyone have paper and a pen?" Paula pulled a hotel notepad from her purse, and I contributed my hotel pen from my shirt breast pocket. "Write down your name, your employee number, and your emergency contact information. Then pass the paper and pen around." He continued, "NOBODY is to leave this group, unless you have an emergency need to use the toilet. You go and immediately return. The restrooms in the mall are open for us to use. Check with the soldiers at the door to the mall; they're letting people in two at a time." Now that it was possible to do so, I REALLY had to use the restroom! "Furthermore," Sam told us, "the attack is NOT over." Having thought only the Trident-Oberoi had been hit, I was stunned to hear Sam say, "The violence wasn't confined to our hotel. The whole city is under attack. Martial law has been declared, and only military transports are on the streets. We're not going anywhere at the moment, people."

When the paper came to me, I dutifully wrote down my information, but I paused at my emergency contact data. I knew my parents were with my sister in Michigan celebrating Thanksgiving, but I didn't know her number or their mobile numbers by heart. So I wrote my parents' home number in faraway Ashtabula, Ohio. Although I had my mobile phone with me, it had my Dutch SIM card, not my US SIM card. The Dutch card only had the numbers of my friends in Amsterdam; my US card was in the luggage I'd left behind in my hotel room. Without the US SIM card, I didn't have access to the phone numbers that linked me to the US. Technology!

Once Sam had the complete list in his hands, he immediately called Richard in Minneapolis. "Richard! Six flight attendants just showed up! They're alive!" he said, relieved and thankful. Turning to the room full of worried TIA staff, Richard whooped, "Six flight attendants just got to the garage! That's everyone!! They're all alive!" Sam could hear the cheers and applause coming through his phone. "Sam," exclaimed Richard, "we've heard from Captain Daniel and Tony Park! They're still barricaded in their hotel rooms, alive and unharmed! We've now accounted for the whole crew!" As Sam repeated the good news about Captain Daniel and Tony to the group, tears of relief ran down his cheeks. I'd never seen a pilot cry; I didn't know they could! Returning to Richard, Sam read off the list of who was in the garage, providing our employee numbers and our emergency contact information. Scattered gunfire still sounded in the distance.

Listening to the news, Colleen looked around, seeing nothing. David, too, was lost in his own world. Finally feeling somewhat safe, Fola began to relax.

After ending the call with Richard, Sam took a moment to wipe away his tears then continued with his briefing. "Since the attack appears to be ongoing, we might have to make a sudden escape. Be prepared to leave any bags behind and keep ON YOUR PERSON anything you'd need if we have to make a run for it, like your passports and crew IDs." Patting my uniform pants' pockets, I confirmed I had already stuffed both items in the pockets of my trousers. "We're not safe yet," warned Sam. "If the terrorists get past the soldiers and come in here shooting, there's really only one way they'd come. That way," he said, pointing toward the open space by the apartment buildings. "That half wall is our only protection from that direction, so crouch down by that wall, keeping your heads below the top of the wall. Stay together. If we have to move, we don't want anyone missing." "I'll go to the restroom now then," I announced. Mary and Paula both decided to go, too. "Go together and come RIGHT back!" instructed Sam. As we rose and walked toward the soldiers at the mall entrance, Ladi joined us. Since the guards were only letting two at a time into the mall, I told Paula and Mary to go first. When they returned, Ladi and I took our turn while the women waited for us at the mall entrance. Walking into the restroom, Ladi looked at me, shaking his head in disbelief at the whole situation. As the four of us returned to the group, Mary quietly told me, "Two women were in front of the ladies' room; they were front desk clerks, and they said at least two of the other front desk clerks were killed." Each occupied with his or her own thoughts, we silently rejoined our group, huddling behind the half wall in the middle of this terrifying night. The temperature was warm, but we all felt chilled to our very souls.

~ ~ ~

Richard and the others at TIA in Minneapolis were busy brainstorming, trying to figure out how they could evacuate us from Mumbai. With the city under martial law and hundreds of people stranded, neither the police nor the army could concern themselves with ferrying a few TIA crew members to the airport. Richard began to investigate other, more extreme options. Over the phone he suggested to Sam that one considered option was to hire a helicopter to land on the garage roof and fly us out to safety! That option excited me a little as I'd never ridden in a helicopter, but in the same moment I wondered what would happen to Ladi and Fola in that case. In the warm Mumbai night we continued to wait.

Raj Kansupada dropped the phone into the cradle at his podium in the Mumbai airport and took off running down the jet bridge at full speed to Flight 36. Startled by the heavy footfalls running toward the plane, Captain Marvin jumped up, heading to the door while he shouted to his crew, "Stay back!" Certain that terrorists were about to storm the plane he felt the hair stand up on the back of his neck. The sleeping crew members woke with their hearts pounding, imagining the worst. Waving the crew list above his head as he ran, Raj exuberantly shouted, "Some of the crew are alive! I just got word some escaped the hotel and survived!!" "WHO?" Debra demanded. "I don't know! Minneapolis just called and told me some have escaped! They didn't want to tell me who yet, there's still much confusion downtown." Some, but not all, thought Samantha. Who is alive? Who might be dead? Those terrible questions hung like a cloud over the exhausted crew. Seeing their reaction and realizing not only what he'd said but how he'd said it, Raj explained, "They're not all lost! There's hope!" Tears again spilled from Samantha's eyes as she thought about what Raj had said. Were the survivors injured? How badly? Even worse, would they be bringing back bodies in the cargo hold? She walked to a seat alone in main cabin, buried her face in her hands, and sobbed.

Taking a deep breath, Raj continued, "Minneapolis is going to make reservations for you, probably at the Airport Hotel. As soon as I have the details, I'll let you know. You'll most likely be leaving once you've gotten some rest." Anne sighed in relief. At least they'd get off the plane, she thought. With its tanks full of fuel and an American flag on its tail.

~ ~ ~

As we sat on the concrete ramp, I tried to take our minds off the situation. "What kind of work do you do?" I asked Ladi and Fola. "I'm an attorney specializing in the oil industry," answered Fola. Ladi said, "I'm an oil company executive. We were here conducting an import deal." "Stay with us for now," I told them. "We'll all get out of this together." Ladi smiled and nodded.

We hadn't been in the alley for long when suddenly, no more than two meters away, something spooked the crowd. In an instant, we were once again in the middle of chaos. I looked down the ramp over the heads of Paula and Mary, scanning the crowd in the alley. The garage lights were ample and just two or three meters from our group I saw a man with a crazed look in his eyes running through the alley right behind Paula, Mary, and Nicolas. All at once, the crowd of evacuees in the garage and alley began to run, creating a stampede. Adrenaline coursing through me, I jumped to my feet, reacting to the perceived danger. Colleen, too, bolted to her feet. I turned to look at her, and my mind registered the strangest thought, *Fascinating. She's still so very feminine.*

Startled, Mary saw me rise, and she turned to look at the crowd behind her. Juan, seeing the commotion, scrambled to his feet. An Indian woman in a sari fell, and people simply ran or jumped over her. It was painful to know we couldn't save her and ourselves, so we turned to run, hoping we wouldn't be trampled in the mindless stampede. Sheer panic took over in the crowd and people began running for the far exit of the alley in an attempt to escape perceived danger approaching from the entrance we'd used. My eyes registered only fleeting freeze-frame images: Ladi jumped up, grabbing Fola by the arms to pull her up off the floor. I sprang up and half jumped-half ran up the ramp away from the stampede. Colleen was only one or two steps behind me. Commanding myself to stop and help the others, I turned to look back. Colleen was moving in a fear-fueled daze, gasping as she struggled to run up the ramp in her high heels, clutching at the bodice of her uniform. Taking a step towards Colleen and Fola, I blindly reached out and grabbed Colleen by her uniform sleeve, while my other hand unsuccessfully tried to hold onto Fola. I don't think Colleen was even aware I had a hold on her. We managed several running steps up the ramp when the soldiers guarding the crowd began blowing whistles and shouting commands in Hindi. In an instant, the crowd slowed and settled down. I could still feel the adrenaline as I watched Colleen take short, labored breaths. We stopped at the top of the ramp at the second floor staring at the soldiers, the crowd, and the rest of our crew, all of whom were on their feet. The Indian woman who fell and was trampled struggled to get up. Nicolas extended his hand to help her. The whole episode was over in a few seconds.

I stood still, Colleen's sleeve still in my hand. Fola and Ladi clung to each other's hands. Soldiers walked by, speaking in Hindi and motioning us to sit back down. Colleen, Fola and Ladi, the others, and I stepped back to the group and sat down. With a pained expression and a sigh of relief, Sam addressed the reassembled group, "THAT is why we need to stay together, everybody! If that happens again, STAY TOGETHER!" Permitting myself my one and only moment of self-pity, I wondered if this nightmare would ever end. The warm, clear night surrounded us, punctuated by the continuing sounds of the attack.

~ ~ ~

After Raj had gone back into the terminal, Captain Marvin told his crew, "Looks like the decision's been made. We're going to a hotel, and the airline is making the arrangements now." The exhausted crew listened in relief. "Gather your things so we can leave the minute we get the hotel details." He turned to the flight deck to get his belongings. Anne, Debra, and Samantha, along with the rest of the crew, collected their luggage. As Debra and Samantha collected their luggage near the front main-cabin galley, Samantha looked toward the service carts then smiled at Debra exchanging a knowing look. "YES!" Debra giggled, as they quickly gathered and stuffed several miniature liquor bottles and a can of beer each in their crew bags. "We certainly need it!" Samantha decided. Under normal circumstances, a crew member can be terminated for taking liquor from a plane. On this night, no one cared.

~ ~ ~

Brushing dirt off her uniform dress, Mary sat beside Paula on the concrete floor. Despite the hour, around 3:00 am local time, I wasn't at all tired. I actually felt that I was perfectly fine and that, after taking time to have my uniform cleaned, I would return to work. In retrospect, of course, I was operating on sheer adrenaline and wasn't thinking clearly. Nicolas shook his head and said to no one in particular, "I'm taking Christmas off this year!" "I'M taking off Christmas AND New Year's!" responded Paula. "New Year's, too?" Nicolas asked. "After THIS, I'm taking off ALL the time I want!" Paula said, with a profound nod of her head. For some reason, her statement struck me as funny and, despite everything that had happened, I laughed—but I was the only one.

Throughout the night explosions and gunfire sounded around the city. Gunfire erupted in the street near us shortly after the stampede. Wordlessly but determinedly we all quickly ducked below the half-wall that Sam had mentioned in his briefing. For all we knew terrorists were shooting into the space! Fortunately we were able to move away from under the wall after a few moments.

After the stampede and the nearby gunfire, the chaos seemed to taper off. Texting with Minneapolis, Sam learned, and told us, the airline had secured rooms at the Airport Hotel for us, suggesting our stay in Mumbai was being extended. I wondered about my luggage, still—I hoped—in my room at the Trident-Oberoi. "We'll need our luggage if we're going to stay here," I told Sam. He responded, "Forget about the luggage. The hotel's on fire. The luggage is gone. When we get out of here, you can buy whatever you'll need." I was unhappy to hear that. Retrieving my luggage seemed both normal and necessary. I actually felt out of sorts realizing I wouldn't see my luggage again...particularly because both my tube of toothpaste and facial cleanser were brand new! I'd kept my life during a terrorist attack, remaining relatively calm, and here I was unhappy about losing easily replaceable toiletries! It's strange and funny how minds work in a crisis, isn't it?! With a sigh, I resigned myself to reality; we'd escaped with only the clothes on our backs and computer bags or purses. We were alive; that was the important thing, the thing to remember. But I still missed my toiletry kit!

~ ~ ~

The first rays of sunlight were beginning to illuminate Mumbai when Raj entered Flight 36's plane. He told the crew, "It's time to go. The airline has rooms for you at the Airport Hotel across the street from the airport." "Everyone, get your things and let's go," ordered a relieved Captain Marvin, leaving no room for argument. Anne, Debra, Samantha, and the rest of the crew gathered at the plane's door. "Stay together," instructed Captain Marvin, leading the way up the jet bridge and into the terminal. Debra walked with her head down, tears shining in her eyes and falling gently onto the bodice of her uniform, emotional exhaustion overtaking her. Samantha took Debra's hand, and the two friends walked together down the quiet terminal corridor.

~ ~ ~

Sam quietly spoke to Ian, and then turned to address the group assembled on the floor. "We're going to a hotel. The airline is considering options to get Tony and Captain Daniel out of the hotel. They might hire a commando squad to free them." "Will they meet us at the hotel later?" asked Mary. "I don't know," answered Sam. "But we can't leave them!" said Mary and Paula in unison. "We all ought to go out together!" I added. "We're all in this together!" Patiently surveying the group, Sam said, "They're stuck in the hotel for now. We can't get them out. I know TIA will get them out as soon as they can, as soon as it's SAFE to get them out of the hotel. But we're already out, and we can't stay here indefinitely." He gestured around the garage and added, "While we have a chance to get further away, to someplace safer, we will. That's just common sense."

We couldn't argue; he was right, I realized. While the attack had apparently abated, it could suddenly rekindle. If it did, we could be trapped in the garage, and that was only slightly better than being trapped in the hotel. "We'll go to the hotel," Sam repeated, "and wait there for Tony and Captain Daniel." At that moment, Sam's phone chimed, signifying another text from Minneapolis. I looked at Ladi and Fola, wondering what they would do. Suddenly, a murmur in the crowd caught my attention.

~ ~ ~

The crew of Flight 36 checked into the Airport Hotel. The hotel was functional, though not as posh as the Trident-Oberoi. Captain Marvin gathered his crew and gave them instructions. "Everybody, write your room numbers on this paper. Stay INSIDE this hotel. I need to be able to get ahold of you, so NO wandering around outside. Order whatever you want from room service or go to the hotel restaurant; call home, use the Internet...whatever. TIA's paying for all of it right now."

Samantha wrote down her room number and said to Debra, "I'm going to try to take a nap. Let's see about lunch later." Debra nodded, feeling an odd mixture of relief and nagging fear. Exhausted, the crew crowded into elevators to go to their rooms.

Daylight showed through the picture windows at the front of the hotel. On the street, traffic hummed. Voices echoed as Mumbai awakened to Thursday, November 27, as if nothing had happened.

Looking out her hotel room window, Anne was struck by how normal everything looked. After the nightmare events of the past night,

Mumbai seemed like business as usual. Life went on. Too wound up to sleep, she took a shower, donned her street clothes, and went downstairs to the restaurant for breakfast, thinking something warm would help her relax and eventually get to sleep.

~ ~ ~

The murmur in the crowd was caused by an announcement being made in Hindi. I saw hotel employees gathering around someone, presumably a manager, who began to brief them. People in civilian clothes began to move toward the entrance of the alley, which was still blocked by soldiers. Seeing my expression, Ladi said, "It's daylight. That means they're probably letting people leave." Realizing he was correct, I responded, "Yes, I see." Off to my right a woman's voice asked, "Are you airline crew?" "Yes!" I exclaimed, and Sam added "Yes. What's going on?" "I'm an off-duty hotel manager here to help," explained the woman. "We have a bus to take you out of here." "Great. Thank you. My airline has reserved rooms for us at the Airport Hotel near the airport," Sam told her.

"Would anyone like some water?" offered the woman. "I only have five bottles; do you mind sharing?" Gratefully, I accepted one, turning to offer some to Ladi and Fola, who declined. The space was clearing out as people left the alley. Gathering our group, Sam said, "Come on, everybody; we're going." Nodding at Ladi and Fola, Sam said to me, "Say goodbye to them." My expression didn't hide my emotions. "We'll be fine," said Ladi, as he and Fola stood to see me off. We shook hands and, through tears, I said, "I'll contact you as soon as I get back to the US." I hated saying goodbye to them. Having survived the attack and the night in the garage together, it was painful to leave them. Their business cards secure in my wallet, I waved one last goodbye to them and joined the rest of my crew gathering at the alley entrance.

~ ~ ~

On the upper floor of the garage, Regina, Katrin, Heidi, and Nina assembled with their crew, ready to leave the garage. Regina prayed that our crew was safe. Her cell battery was now dead, so she couldn't text Lutz. She knew, though, that he'd be waiting for her at home. Still holding tight to Katrin, Nina looked back and forth expecting more terrifying sights. Heidi, still separated from her Alpine International crew, stayed with the German crew, simply glad to be getting out. Across the alley at another exit, a bus waited for them.

While all of Regina's crew was together, half of the other Frankfurt GIA crew was missing, as was most of the other Munich GIA crew. They were still trapped in the hotel, barricaded in rooms they were afraid to leave, like Captain Daniel and Tony Park, until liberated by the military. Two members of the Frankfurt crew were in the attack at Leopold Cafe; they staggered back to the hotel only to find that under siege as well. Eventually, they found their way to the others in the garage. One of them, a woman flight attendant, was injured. Grazed by a bullet at Leopold Cafe, she had been bandaged up as best as possible under the circumstances. Once she and her companion made it to the garage, she let the waves of shock roll over her.

As she walked away from the garage, Regina looked back with a mixture of exhaustion and relief. Grateful to be leaving and very glad the attack seemed to be over, she took a window seat in the bus. She knew that...someday...she'd return to Mumbai. Nina was still terrified and remained close by Katrin's side. "We're going to another hotel," the de facto captain told them. "They have someplace for the crew. The inbound crews have gone to a suburban hotel. They'll be flying us out this evening." Regina wanted a drink of water; she wanted sleep. Exhausted, she leaned her head against the window, closed her eyes, and—for the first time since the attack began—sighed in relief.

~ ~ ~

Managers from the Trident-Oberoi buzzed around the garage and gathered hotel guests. Ladi and Fola joined a group of guests from Italy, Japan, and the United Kingdom who were being moved to a different hotel. Taxis, surrounded by police cars, were assembled by the back exit from the alley. In short order, Ladi and Fola were in a taxi bound for another hotel. For the first time since the attack began, Fola didn't try to stop her tears. The 30-minute drive to the safe hotel was a blur as Fola cried in relief.

~ ~ ~

As we approached the bus taking us away from the garage, I noticed it was the same one in which we'd left the airport more than 24 hours earlier and a lifetime ago. We all got on the bus: Ian, Nicolas, Colleen, me, Juan, Paula, Mary, David, and finally Sam. All the shades were drawn. "Stay toward the center of the bus," Sam instructed. "If there's still anything going on, shots may be fired. Keep the shades closed; no one needs to see us or know where we're going." The off-duty hotel manager who had brought us out of the garage to the bus spoke to the driver in Hindi and then turned to us. "I'm so sorry this happened to you. Have a safe trip home." I waved to her; she waved back and got off the bus. With a jolt, the bus pulled away from the garage and into the deserted, debris-strewn street. Bright daylight shone through the front windows of the bus and peeked through the edges of the shades. Colleen, seated in front of me, leaned her head back and closed her eyes. Seated on the aisle floor, Sam texted Minneapolis letting them know we were out of the garage and on our way to the Airport Hotel. We were all silent; the events of the night replaying themselves in our minds.

As we gained speed, I peeked out of the window around the edge of the shade. It was an odd sight: the city was deserted, there was no traffic, and no one was outside. I began to see people clustered in windows and doorways, watching from safety. The full scope of the attack was absolutely shocking. Mumbai was still under martial law, and we were escaping from a war zone. For us it was finally over—and on American Thanksgiving itself, of all days! We were certainly thankful.

~ ~ ~

Still barricaded with Paul and Umesh, Tony learned from Minneapolis by phone that the rest of us had been evacuated from the garage and were on our way to the Airport Hotel. While Tony was glad to hear that news, he was still fearful. Looking out at the city through the crack between the curtains, Tony wondered how much longer he'd have to wait to be rescued. The three men were rationing food and water as they waited.

~ ~ ~

Hearing we were out of the garage and safe from Richard in Minneapolis, Captain Daniel felt a rush of relief. He then called Tony. Umesh answered the phone, and then passed the phone to Tony. Daniel assured Tony he was not alone and that, when they could leave, they would leave together. He also assured Tony that they'd frequently speak from now on as they hadn't spoken during the worst of the attack. Tony bravely assured Captain Daniel that he was holding up OK, and Captain Daniel resolved to call Tony frequently. With the television sound off, Captain Daniel watched the Mumbai morning news. Seeing the grizzly scenes of carnage fill the screen, he was actually glad he couldn't hear the description of the death and destruction; the images were bad enough.

~ ~ ~

Ladi and Fola were impressed with their new accommodations in a suburban mall setting near the airport. However, they didn't have any toiletries or clean clothes. Fola turned on the television; seeing the images of Mumbai under attack, she immediately turned it off. Ladi suggested, "Let's lie down for a nap and then decide what to do." Still dressed in the sweats they'd rapidly donned when the attack first began, they tried to get a bit of sleep on this hot morning in Mumbai.

~ ~ ~

As our bus pulled up to the Airport Hotel, Sam said, "Let me check out the situation first. You all stay here until I return." He stepped out into the bright sunlight of a morning in Mumbai and looked up at the façade of the hotel. He was greeted by hotel employees who escorted him into the building. TIA had secured as many of the hotel's rooms as it could.

Mary looked out, wondering exactly where we were. David, opening his eyes, asked Colleen where we were. "I don't know," she replied. "We're at the Airport Hotel," I chimed in. "Sam's gone to check things out."

In the lobby of the Airport Hotel, Anne was headed to breakfast when she saw Sam. He had spoken with the front desk clerk and was walking toward the door on his way back to the bus. Recognizing Sam as a crew member by his rumpled dirty uniform shirt, Anne rushed up to him and asked, "Are you with TIA? Did you just come from the Trident-Oberoi?" Sam turned to her, his brow furrowing in concern. Anne quickly produced her airline ID and told him she was a flight attendant from TIA's inbound flight. Although they had not previously met, without a word, the two instinctively hugged. While Sam returned to the bus to collect the rest of us, Anne waited at the door, a bit frightened at what she might see. Shading her eyes against the sun, she saw Nicolas framed in the light at the door of the bus.

~ ~ ~

Regina, Katrin, Nina, and the rest arrived at another suburban hotel. Individual rooms were unavailable, but the hotel did its best to accommodate the more than 25 refugees. Some cots and bedding were set up in a conference room. In another, a buffet breakfast awaited. They were all told that GIA would cover any expenses, like toiletries and food from the gift shop. Regina bought a toothbrush and a trial-sized tube of toothpaste. She and the others bedded down on the cots, trying to nap. Exhausted, Regina quickly nodded off. An additional 15 GIA crew members awaited rescue from the devastated Trident-Oberoi Hotel.

~ ~ ~

Throughout the Trident-Oberoi and downtown Mumbai, the attack continued to sporadically flare up. The fire that had been set in the Oberoi side of the hotel complex was extinguished overnight. The military SWAT troopers began the arduous task of combing the whole facility for terrorists who might still be hiding in the building. Tony and Captain Daniel remained quiet in their respective rooms, as did other hotel guests similarly barricaded. By early Thursday morning, both Tony and Captain Daniel managed to nod off to sleep, since the worst of the attack appeared to be over. The army instructed those trapped in their rooms to remain barricaded until such time as all terrorists were either apprehended or killed. People were safer in their rooms than walking the halls not knowing where the terrorists were holed up.

~ ~ ~

Anne ushered us inside. She reached out, hugged each one of us, and said, "I'm so glad you're here!" We must have looked awful, but she didn't blink. Intuitively, she didn't pepper us with questions. Instead, she automatically went into "mother mode," asking each of us whether we needed to see a doctor or needed medication. At the reception desk, Sam told us the hotel needed time to arrange and clean rooms for us, so he suggested we have breakfast in the hotel restaurant while we waited. "Yes! I'll take them," announced Anne. "Come on," she said, taking Colleen by the hand.

Anne told the restaurant staff that we had been in the attack. "Please help me pull several tables together," she asked the staff. In moments, a line of tables was arranged and we sat down. A waiter brought us menus, and Anne told us to order whatever we wanted because all expenses were being covered by the airline. Waiters brought us each a bottle of cool water. Once we were settled, we sort of just sat there, exhausted, not really able to focus on the menus.

~ ~ ~

In spite of the beautiful sunshine filtering into her room around the curtains, Debra finally slept. Samantha texted with her sister Teresa in the US, assured Teresa she was alright, and eventually nodded off to sleep. No one yet knew exactly when we'd leave Mumbai.

~ ~ ~

Anne encouraged us to drink water and eat. At first, I wasn't at all hungry; after eating a bit of toast, I quickly felt ravenous! Anne listened patiently as we spoke, snippets of our experiences emerging. A well-meaning waiter offered us Mumbai newspapers. In English the headlines screamed the attack, and the cover story included a graphic photo of the Taj Mahal Hotel on fire. David turned away and mumbled, "No, thank you. We lived it!" Ian also waved off a copy. I accepted a copy, and I'm glad I did. I didn't read it at the time, but I eventually did after my return home. It gave me a concise chronology of the attack, along with speculation about the terrorists and their agenda. Much of the information remained unclear at the moment, but the paper detailed much of the massive attack.

I asked a waiter for a second bottle of water to take up to my room; he graciously brought everyone a second bottle. Sam finally joined us and explained that the hotel had arranged for us to stay temporarily in its VIP suite. Sam and Ian returned to the reception desk to continue sorting out rooms while the rest of us headed for the suite. A relieved Anne returned to her room.

The seven of us flight attendants filed into the three-room suite - a large bedroom, a living/dining room, and a fully equipped kitchen. The air conditioning could only minimally assuage Mumbai's tropical heat. We all found a place to sit. Selecting a seat at the dining table, I retrieved my laptop and turned it on. Colleen sat on the sofa. She was quiet and, despite the warmth and humidity, she kept her uniform sweater tightly wrapped around herself. Mary sank into a wing chair, utterly exhausted, and David sat in the chair next to her. Juan absent-mindedly rifled through the kitchen.

~ ~ ~

My laptop picked up the hotel's WIFI signal, but I couldn't access the Internet. The system required both the room number and the guest's last name. I called the hotel operator to register myself so I could go online. We weren't individually registered, though, so the operator couldn't provide the necessary information. I quickly grew exasperated and angry. We had just been through a terrorist attack, and I wanted to contact family and friends back home. This ridiculous technicality was preventing me, and I lost patience. Now, I admit I'm not the most technologically adept, but this seemed completely ridiculous. I finally hung up on the operator, in utter disgust at her inability or unwillingness to help me. I realized I was probably stressed from the night's experience. Totally fed up, I turned off my computer to conserve its battery. While I had the computer's electrical cord it wouldn't work with India's power outlets without an electrical adapter and mine was in my lost crew luggage. Paula turned on the television but, after the sights and sounds of the attack flew across the screen, Nicolas quietly said, "Turn that off, please." Warm sunshine filtered into the room.

Sam and Ian joined us about 30 minutes later. We were all beginning to show signs of the stress we'd been under, and we weren't our usual selves. I was angry, for nonspecific reasons. Colleen was stoically silent, with no sign of her usual bubbly disposition. Juan continued to pace around the room, poking at the furnishings. "They have a few rooms for us," announced Sam. "But we'll have to share. You ladies will all stay here in this suite, and Ian and I will share a room. The rest of you, work that out among yourselves. We don't yet know when we're leaving Mumbai. Figure out the rooms so I can write down where you are. DO NOT leave the hotel for ANY reason!! I'll call each room to let you know when to meet. Juan and David took a key, leaving one for me and Nicolas." "You take it, Doug," said Nicolas, "I'll wait here." Seething in anger, I managed to hold my temper. We had once dated, and I wanted to shout at him that he needn't worry I'd molest him if we were in the same room. A knock on the door interrupted my mental outburst. Sam answered it, and the clerk handed him another key to a room that had just become available. "Here," said Sam, handing the key to Nicolas. "There. Everybody has a room." He quickly wrote down the names and room numbers. "Buy whatever you need from the gift shop and charge it to your room. Use the Internet. Go to the restaurant. Have whatever you want from the mini-bar. TIA's paying for everything," said Sam. "But stay IN THE HOTEL," he cautioned us again. Computer bag in hand, I took my leave, trudging off to my room on the fourth floor.

~ ~ ~

Fola tossed and turned, unable to sleep. She finally got up. Using the complimentary hotel toiletries, she brushed her teeth and washed her face. Hearing Fola in the bathroom, Ladi awoke from his light sleep. Fola sat next to him on the bed and said quietly, "I want to go home; I need to see our children." Together they went downstairs to the travel agency in the hotel. The agent was very helpful, profusely apologizing on behalf of the Indian people for the attack. Ladi and Fola thanked her and explained that they wanted to return to Nigeria as soon as possible. After consulting her computer, the agent broke the bad news. Not only would a considerable charge be incurred to change their tickets, but that night's flight from Mumbai to Lagos was sold out.

The travel agent called Air Nigeria directly to inquire if there was anything they could do to return a Nigerian couple home as soon as possible after a terrorist attack. Air Nigeria agreed to waive the change fee, but they couldn't make empty seats appear on that night's sold-out flight. It could, however, confirm them on its flight to Lagos out of Delhi that night, if Ladi and Fola could get to Delhi in time. In short order, the agent booked Ladi and Fola onto a domestic flight to Delhi that left in just three hours. Poorer by $500, Ladi and Fola caught a cab to the airport, on their way home after a night they'd never forget.

~ ~ ~

At their hotel, after her brief nap, Regina nibbled at breakfast but wasn't able to eat very much. The hotel had closed its gymnasium and pool for the day to enable the GIA crew members' sole access to the locker room and shower facilities. Supplying the crew as best it could, the gift shop sold out its entire stock of toothbrushes and had to send out for more. An inbound GIA flight had arrived during the attack; they were notified that, as soon as they had completed the mandatory layover time, they would fly back to Frankfurt with the crew members who had been in the attack. The GIA captain who'd organized the crew members in the garage instructed Heidi to call Alpine International Airlines to let them know she was safe and that she would fly to Frankfurt with the GIA crew members when they left Mumbai.

Returning to the cots with Katrin and Nina, who would not leave Katrin's side, Regina worried about the GIA crew still trapped in the hotel, as well as "the Americans," our TIA crew. "They got out of the hotel with us, Regina," Katrin reminded her. "They're safe, somewhere." On a cot near Katrin and Nina, Regina finally managed to nap a little more in the hot afternoon.

~ ~ ~

Colleen curled up on the couch in the living room of the suite and was finally able to sleep. Mary drew the drapes. She and Paula undressed down to their slips and each took a bed in the bedroom. They all managed to drift off into a fitful sleep. After about two hours, Colleen was started awake by the sounds of housekeeping staff in the hallway. She sat up in panic, screaming "NO! NO! NO!" while looking around the room in panic and terror. Hearing Colleen, Paula and Mary both woke up. Mary stumbled toward Colleen calling calmly, "It's alright, Colleen. It's OK. It's all over." Colleen visibly relaxed as Mary took her hand. "Oh, God," Colleen blinked, sitting up. "I need a glass of water." "Let me get it for you," Mary offered. As she took a bottle of water from the mini-bar and poured it into a cup for Colleen, Mary caught sight of herself in a mirror. Her trademark ponytail was a wreck, and she had dark circles under her eyes. "We're alive," she reminded herself aloud. "Here, hon," she said, handing Colleen the water. "We're alright, Colleen. We'll be home soon." Colleen nodded, staring into the distance.

~ ~ ~

Once in my room, I turned on the television and set up my computer. This time, thankfully, I was able to quickly connect to the Internet by accepting the charges to my room. I wanted to e-mail the people to whom I was the closest, but I couldn't decide exactly whom I wanted to tell at the moment. I decided to definitely e-mail my brother Andy and his wife Urska in Missouri, who wouldn't see the email until Thursday morning the 27th, along with the three men in Chicago I consider my "chosen brothers": Joee, Don, and Rob. Then I thought of Joanne and hesitated a moment. Prior to our altercation, I wouldn't have thought twice about telling her anything. Now wasn't the time to worry about nonsense so I disregarded our recent tension and included her in the e-mail. That e-mail shook the world of my friends. Here's exactly what I wrote, with the subject line "From Doug URGENT EMERGENCY":

"Am in Mumbai (Bombay) India. There was a terrorist attack on hotel, many killed and injured. Escaped hotel amid gunfire, fire, and bombs. I'm OK, but have lost everything including my cell phone. Will contact you when I get back to the USA. Love Doug."

There, I thought, as I pressed the SEND key. *That will do until I get home.* Being in a rather traumatized state and not thinking clearly, I honestly thought that single e-mail would be the end of the issue until I got home to Chicago. Little did I know what I was setting in motion!

At that time of year, Mumbai is 10.5 hours ahead of Chicago, so Thursday morning, November 27, in Mumbai was Wednesday night, November 26, in Chicago. Joanne was in her home office at her computer when my e-mail chimed through at about 10:30 pm. When she read it, Joanne immediately went to CNN's website and also turned on the small television next to her computer. CNN.com was the better resource, and she stared in horror at the images from Mumbai. Responding to my e-mail, she quickly typed, "Oh my God honey! Are you alright? Is there ANYTHING I can do? Love you!" She thanked the Universe that our last communication, before I'd left on this trip sequence, ended with us both typing the words "I love you." Some of the addresses on my e-mail were mutual friends of ours, and she decided that—despite the lateness of the hour—she would phone them in case they hadn't been at their computers to receive my e-mail. All the calls went to voicemail, so she left messages.

~ ~ ~

Aboard the Indian domestic flight to Delhi, Fola and Ladi realized how dehydrated they were and asked the flight attendants for several cups of water. Arriving at Delhi International Airport with time to spare before their flight home to Lagos, they ate a quick meal and drank more liquids. The flight was full, but Ladi and Fola didn't care. As the 747 lifted off the runway, they held hands, their eyes shining with tears, as they praised the glory of God and said prayers of thanksgiving to Him for sparing their lives.

~ ~ ~

Staring at the complimentary toiletries in the bathroom, I decided the toothpaste, razor, soap, and shampoo would do. Nothing in the mini-bar appealed to me, and I'm not a coffee drinker. I knew the hotel's gift shop carried Diet Coke®, but what I really craved was a proper Diet Pepsi®. While I was considering my options, I heard my computer chime with an e-mail; it was from Joanne. I clicked REPLY, but it seemed the hotel's WIFI was too slow. In exasperation, I composed a new e-mail. I repeated that I was safe and unhurt, and asked her to try to reach my brother Andy if she could locate his phone number. Thanks to modern technology, with phone numbers stored on our phones, I didn't know Andy's number by heart, nor did I know Joanne's. Those phone numbers were on my phone's US SIM card; the card was in my luggage at the Trident-Oberoi. I told Joanne on what street Andy lived and, if she reached Andy, told her to ask him to call our parents. The effects of shock are insidious, and—in retrospect—my thinking really wasn't very clear. Without an address book or my US contact list, I felt completely adrift.

After sending my second e-mail to Joanne, I turned off my computer, concerned about conserving its battery. Using the hotel toiletries, I was able to take a much-needed shower and brush my teeth. As the day was beautifully warm and sunny, I actually thought about going out to the hotel's pool, but realizing I didn't have a swimsuit or flip flops, I immediately negated the idea. Instead, I stripped out of my filthy uniform, took a shower, then utterly exhausted and completely wrung out, collapsed into bed and immediately fell asleep.

We were all reaching out, calling home. Sam phoned his wife, and TIA in Minneapolis. David called his wife Sharon, and Juan called his mother.

~ ~ ~

When Joanne opened my second e-mail with more details about my brother, Andy, she immediately tried to locate his contact information online. Andy is a police officer, so his phone number is unlisted as a safety precaution. Joee has some excellent resources, so Joanne phoned him again to enlist his help in locating Andy. She left the information she had on Andy in Joee's voicemail and asked Joee to call her in the morning. She turned off her computer and the television, and went to bed, grateful I was safe. She drifted off to sleep, the bloody images of Mumbai dancing in her nightmares.

~ ~ ~

TIA made final arrangements to get the two crews at the Airport Hotel out of Mumbai. Captain Marvin, from the inbound TIA flight, was told they would be leaving the hotel at 6:00 pm to fly back to Amsterdam. Since all the crew members had been ordered to remain in the hotel, he decided to let them sleep; everyone was exhausted. Setting his alarm for 4:00 pm, he nodded off to sleep.

~ ~ ~

Joee checked his voicemail late when he and his partner, Scott, returned home that Wednesday night. Listening to it, he shrieked, and Scott rushed to his side. "What is it?" Scott asked. Leaning his elbows on the table and placing his head in his hands, Joee said miserably, "Doug's been in a terrorist attack. He's in INDIA! India! How do we get him out of there??" Scott raced to the television, tuning it to CNN. Watching the horrible images from Mumbai, Scott turned white. Gulping, he turned to Joee, took a deep breath, and quavered, "Is Doug alive?" Tears in his eyes, Joee blurted, "Yes, thank God! And he says he's OK. He sent an e-mail to several of us, and Joanne called me in case

I didn't see the e-mail immediately." Letting out an audible sigh, Scott said, "He's alive, Joee; he'll get out. Doug's got what it takes to survive."

Joee immediately contacted his resources and succeeded in locating Andy's police station. He called the station at about 1:00 am. Andy was escorting a suspected drunk driver to the station's holding facility when he heard the station dispatcher page him over the PA system. Turning the drunk over to another officer, Andy went to the dispatcher's desk.

Looking up from her switchboard the dispatcher asked, "Do you have a brother, Doug O'Keeffe?" The hair stood up on Andy's neck, and for a moment he lost his usual police officer's composure. Fearing the worst but forcing himself to remain calm, he replied, "Yes. What's wrong?" "We've received an emergency message from a friend of his in Chicago. Your brother is OK, but he was in a terrorist attack." Andy grabbed his pen as the dispatcher gave him Joee's name and phone number. Neither he nor the dispatcher had heard any news coverage since they'd come on shift at 11:00 pm. Andy didn't know I was in India; he only knew I was flying. Worried and anxious, Andy resolved to find out more information before contacting our parents, who were celebrating Thanksgiving with our sister's family in Michigan.

~ ~ ~

A few minutes after 3:00 pm on Thursday in Mumbai, I was awakened by a knock on my hotel room door by a housekeeper wanting to know if I needed to have my room cleaned. Miserable and groggy, I declined. I realized that no news had reached me about leaving, and I wondered whether I'd missed the phone call. The message light on the phone was not illuminated, but I picked up the handset to ensure the phone was working. Hearing the dial tone, I sighed. No news yet. Then I opened the curtains to let the bright afternoon sunshine into the dim room.

~ ~ ~

Downstairs in the VIP suite, Colleen had more water from the mini bar and looked around. Before the attack, she had showered, brushed her teeth, and dressed in her clean uniform; that felt like a lifetime ago. Her uniform was now a wrinkled mess, and her breath reminded her she didn't have a toothbrush. Quietly letting herself out of the room, Colleen hurried to the hotel's gift shop to buy a few toiletries. Looking out the windows of the hotel's lobby, she saw everyday people doing everyday things in the bright sunshine and tropical heat. She knew that life goes on, even after a crisis, but she still found herself amazed at the ordinary activities around her. *How strange*, she thought. *Don't they know what happened?* Mumbai went about its business, but for Colleen the world would never be the same.

~ ~ ~

Still barricaded in their rooms at the Trident-Oberoi, Captain Daniel and Tony Park were able to use the hotel phones. It still wasn't safe to leave their rooms, and they heard occasional random noises that suggested an ongoing military assault on the terrorists remaining in the hotel. Minneapolis kept both of them informed about what was happening. In case terrorists were listening in, callers used codes to tell of our safety in another hotel and to explain the ongoing actions.

The Indian Special Forces were preparing to launch a final attack against the terrorists. By midafternoon on Thursday the hotel's utilities were to be shut off in preparation for the attack. This would cut the terrorists off from any outside communication, direction, or organization. The soldiers knew where Captain Daniel and Tony were located, but they didn't want to take any chances. Captain Daniel and Tony were told to remain hidden in their rooms. More than 100 people remained trapped in the hotel, many still in their rooms. The terrorists had been defeated elsewhere; the Trident-Oberoi and the Taj Mahal hotels were the final terrorist holdouts.

~ ~ ~

Sighing at the lack of Diet Pepsi®, I grudgingly settled for a Diet Coke® from my room's mini-fridge and sat down at my computer, wondering what had transpired while I slept. Joanne had awakened several times during the night to check her e-mail and to send me encouraging messages. Next I saw two e-mails from Joee.

In Chicago a few minutes before 2:00 am, Joee's phone rang. Jolted out of a fitful sleep on the couch, Joee gasped a hello. "This is Andrew Lenart calling about my brother, Doug O'Keeffe," said Andy, unsure to whom he was speaking. "This is Joee Arteaga, Doug's best friend in Chicago. Doug asked me to call; he's been in a terrorist attack." Assuming Andy hadn't heard about the attack, Joee continued, "He's in Mumbai, India, and there's been a major terrorist attack." "India?!" Andy asked, surprised. "I didn't know he was flying there." "Doug sent an e-mail telling us there was an attack at the hotel, that he escaped the hotel under gunfire, and that the hotel had been set on fire," Joee finished. His emotions in turmoil, Andy caught his breath before managing to ask, "Has he been shot? Is he alright?" "Yes, he's alright. Sorry, I should have said that first. He hasn't been hurt at all," answered Joee. Andy breathed a heavy sigh of relief. "Doug's been in contact with a mutual friend, and I've e-mailed him but haven't gotten a response yet," said Joee. "He's lost everything. To me, that means he dropped everything and ran; I know I would have! He's definitely lost his phone and probably also his passport." Andy paused and said quietly, "Oh, my God. I love him so much. I can't imagine him not being here!" Then he exclaimed, "You know, I'm jealous! He's sharing information with you that could help save his life but he's not telling us!"

Knowing that Andy hadn't seen any of the news coverage, Joee paused and said, "When he got to the hotel where he is now, he probably only had a few minutes at a computer to e-mail whomever he could. He probably e-mailed you but you haven't seen it yet." Thinking of the time difference, Andy realized that was probably an accurate guess, and he relaxed a bit. "What can we do?" He asked Joee, truly feeling lost. "If everything is gone, we might need a copy of his birth certificate to prove citizenship." Thinking aloud, Joee said, "Doug did ask for you to contact your parents. Please ask them if they have a copy of his birth certificate when you call. Keep your phone on and save my number. I promise I'll call you with anything I hear and let's plan to speak in the morning." "I work until 7:00 am," Andy told Joee. "I'm going to call the family after I get off work, then I have to get some sleep because I work tomorrow night, too." The two concluded the call with promises to call each other with any new information. Andy returned to work, shouldering a heavy burden of worry, and Joee went to sleep.

~ ~ ~

Early Thanksgiving morning, Joanne's phone rang. Caller ID told her Joee was calling. "Did you get ahold of Andy?" she asked. "Yes, and I e-mailed Doug. We'll get him out and home," Joee said confidently, and he relayed his conversation with Andy. "I'm supposed to spend Thanksgiving and the rest of the weekend with friends in the suburbs because I have a wedding rehearsal on Friday night (Joanne was going to be a wedding officiant). I assume Doug will fly into O'Hare Airport. Let me know the details, and I'll meet you all at the airport if I'm not in the middle of the wedding rehearsal." She gave Joee her cell phone number and instructed, "I'll keep checking my e-mail and my cell. Call me the second you hear ANYTHING." "Will do," promised Joee, but unfortunately he didn't keep his promise to Joanne.

~ ~ ~

In Mumbai, I was beginning to think a bit more clearly although I was still exhausted. I answered Joanne's e-mails, telling her I was alright and I'd speak with her when I got home. Even though she had put her home and cell phone numbers in her e-mail, I wasn't clear-headed enough to phone her. Seeing Joee's e-mail that he'd spoken with Andy was a relief. I was glad to know the family had been notified because I knew TIA wouldn't have been able to do so because I couldn't give them any of my family members' phone numbers. Joee wanted to know when I was due to land at O'Hare Airport so he could pick me up; I didn't know anything yet. Chicago in November was definitely not as warm as tropical Mumbai, so I asked Joee to bring a coat for me to wear when I arrived. However, I failed to ask Joee for his phone number. I learned many a valuable lesson as a result of being in a terrorist attack. One of them is that even people who are not physically injured in a harrowing, shocking event are psychologically traumatized. They can't think clearly, make major decisions, or be aware of details around them. I didn't know it then, but later realized just how traumatized I was...essentially, I was walking wounded.

~ ~ ~

Upon reaching the hotel room he shared with Juan, David felt his adrenaline begin to fade and realized he was both physically sore and exhausted, as well as mentally wrung out. "I can't wait to get home to you, babe," he told Shannon over the phone, "and I'm never coming back here." After stripping down to his underwear and climbing into bed, David tossed and turned, as he listened to Juan's rhythmic breathing, and finally fell asleep.

~ ~ ~

Samantha awoke at 3:00 pm, hungry and dehydrated, squinting at the bright sunshine in her hotel room. She had spent the night worrying about her own safety, the safety of her crew, the safety of my crew, and texting with her sister. It had been an exhausting nine hours. Now, in the relative safety of the Airport Hotel, she was relieved that the danger appeared to be over. She picked up her room phone to order coffee and lunch from room service. She was unaware that the majority of my crew was in the same hotel, safe and sound.

~ ~ ~

After breakfast and seeing us into the VIP suite, Anne collapsed into bed around 9:00 am; she tossed and turned before finally falling asleep. Exhausted, she didn't wake up until Captain Marvin called her at 5:00 pm, telling her to be downstairs in an hour. Glad to be leaving Mumbai, Anne hurried to put on her makeup and pull her hair into something less resembling Medusa!

~ ~ ~

Nicolas got very little sleep. Each time he managed to doze off, some noise or other jolted him awake. His brain was still on high alert.

Eventually realizing sleep wouldn't come, he walked downstairs to the restaurant for coffee. As he left the restaurant with coffee in hand, he saw Colleen in the gift shop. "Are you doing OK?" asked Nicolas. Colleen nodded, still unable to articulate. "Let me walk back with you," he said. At the VIP suite, Colleen reclined on the couch. Nicolas asked, "Do you mind if I sit here with you for a while?" "No, go ahead," she replied. Relaxing in a wing-backed chair, Nicolas stared at the bright sunshine of a beautiful day peeking through the curtains.

~ ~ ~

In the bathroom of the VIP suite Paula shook out her uniform dress, using a washcloth to remove the worst of the garage floor dirt. She brushed her teeth and washed her face. Looking in the mirror, she was taken aback at the bags under her eyes and, for the first time, realized one of her earrings was missing. "DAMN!" She raged at her image. "I liked these earrings!" Angrily she brushed away a few tears.

~ ~ ~

Waking after a solid five hours of sleep, Sam heard Ian in the bathroom. He picked up the room phone and direct-dialed Operations in Minneapolis. He was told that as soon as the—detailed, unbendable, federal—rest requirements were met by Captain Marvin and his crew, they would fly us out of Mumbai that evening. Sam was told to have his crew ready to leave the hotel by 6:00 pm. He hung up the phone and said to Ian, "We're leaving at 6:00 pm. I'll wait to tell the rest of the crew so news won't get out. I'll give them a 30-minute warning." "OK," said Ian. "I'm going downstairs to get something to eat and drink." Sam decided to join him, and the two left the room. In the lobby the big screen televisions were showing the attack carnage in a continuous loop. Seeing that, the men quickly turned away and took their lunches back to their room.

~ ~ ~

In my room, I kept turning my computer on and off to conserve its battery because I didn't think to just buy an electrical converter from the hotel gift shop. The Internet was abuzz with news of the attack, commentary, and speculation. I wish now that I had saved some of that information, but I wasn't thinking clearly. When my room phone rang at 5:30 pm, I knew it had to be someone calling to tell me we were leaving the hotel, and I was right. Sam told me to be downstairs in 30 minutes. "Thanks," I responded, and then I quickly e-mailed Joee that I was on my way home. In my compromised mental state I completely forgot to email Joanne.

~ ~ ~

When my brother, Andy, returned home Thursday morning after work, his wife Urska immediately knew something was wrong. After explaining the situation to her, Andy wanted to wait before calling our parents at our sister's house in Detroit. Urska offered to call the family so Andy could get some sleep, but Andy felt it would be better if he made the call. At about 9:00 am in Detroit, Andy called and spoke to our mother. "Hi there! Happy Thanksgiving!" Mom chirped. "Hi," said Andy, taking a deep breath. "I have some news. Doug's OK, but he's been in a terrorist attack." Mom gasped and called out to our father in a "something is seriously wrong" tone; he hurried over to her side. My sister's children were up and running around with the television blaring cartoons in the background. "We're going upstairs to use the phone, where it's quieter," Mom told my sister.

~ ~ ~

When Debra received the departure phone call, she couldn't dress and get downstairs fast enough. Her one and only thought was to get home. Unaware that our crew was leaving with them, Debra hurried downstairs so she could get some coffee. She saw Samantha and Anne in the lobby. "The crew from the hotel is here!!" Anne announced. "They're in a bit of shock. The attack was very bad. But none of the crew was hurt, thank God!" "Doug's here?" asked Samantha with relief and some trepidation. "Yes," Anne assured her. "He seems fine. From what I've heard so far it was terrible." Debra then happened to see me on the fourth floor balcony.

~ ~ ~

As I looked down at the hotel's busy lobby from the fourth floor balcony, Debra looked up and exclaimed, "DOUG!!" I heard and saw her, but I didn't react. That was odd for me because I was usually an ebullient person. Debra rushed to meet me at the base of the stairs and grabbed me in a big hug. "Oh, Doug!" she cried, as she looked up into my face. "Are you alright??" "Yes, honey, I'm fine," I replied, although my face clearly did not reflect my words. Samantha hurried to hug me, and the two women led me to a seat in the lobby. Samantha was surprised at how composed I looked and that, having been in a bombing, I wasn't a torn and tattered bloody mess. Nicolas waved a greeting from a seat across from me. As I sat, flanked by Debra and Samantha holding my hands, I slowly became aware of the other members of the Flight 36 crew gathering. Then I saw David and Juan enter the lobby, joined a moment later by Colleen, Paula, and Mary. "What happened?" asked Debra quietly. I took a deep breath. Aware of my fellow survivors now within earshot and not wanting to upset anyone, I chose my words carefully, giving the group a synopsis of the events. Debra's face turned almost grey as my words sank in. When I told of the death and devastation in the lobby, Samantha visibly winced and turned away, unable to hear any more. In retrospect, Debra wished she hadn't asked. Colleen remained quiet, sitting away from us so she wouldn't hear me tell our tale.

Anne silently thanked God that she had been spared the worst of the attack, saved by her trade with Mary. Slowly, she approached Mary, asking her if she was alright. Knowing that Anne must feel guilty for having traded the trip sequence that put Mary into the attack, Mary immediately assured Anne she was fine and told her not to feel any burden because of the trade. Breathing a sigh of relief, Anne hugged Mary. Glancing at her reflection in a lobby mirror, Mary realized she had a run in her pantyhose. *Forget it!* she thought to herself. *Today the airline can stuff its appearance standards!*

~ ~ ~

In the lobby, with Captain Marvin on one side and Ian on the other, Sam called out to us, "Everyone! Gather around. We're leaving now. Stay together in the airport and through security. Keep your passports on your person! In the unlikely event anything untoward happens at the airport, RUN to the gas station across the street, and we'll meet up there." "What about Captain Daniel and Tony?" asked Mary; Paula and I immediately chimed in, wanting to know about them, too. Sam answered, "I've spoken with Minneapolis. They're still stuck in the hotel, but they're safe. They can't leave their rooms until the military finishes its sweep for the terrorists." "But we can't leave without them," cried Mary. "Mary," Sam said calmly, "I don't want to leave them either, believe me. But it's going to be at least another day before they get out, and we have to leave while we can get out." Sam paused, hoping Mary would understand the logic. "This is an emergency situation, everyone. As soon as Captain Daniel and Tony can leave the hotel, they'll be flown home. Since we're ready to leave now, we have to go NOW." I knew Sam was right, but I certainly disliked the circumstances.

While the Flight 36 crew members piled their luggage into the belly of the bus, the rest of us stood by holding the meager possessions with which we'd managed to escape. In my computer bag, in addition to my computer and its electrical cord, I had my hotel toothbrush, the newspaper I had received at breakfast, and—inexplicably—two Indian paper prints I had purchased in Mumbai as gifts. I had put them in the computer bag to prevent them from getting bent out of shape in my crew suitcase, and they had survived the ordeal with me. In my well-worn, dirty uniform, I climbed into the bus more than ready to return home—and weirdly relieved that I wouldn't have to work the flight!

~ ~ ~

Tony was devastated when Richard in Minneapolis told him the rest of us were being evacuated. "What about ME?" he demanded. "As soon as it's safe for you and Captain Daniel to leave the hotel, you'll both be flown home," Richard assured Tony. "But we can't take a chance on you leaving the hotel now, while the military are still searching for the terrorists. You're safe in your hotel room, and we've been told the military expects you'll be able to leave in the morning." Disappointed and more than a little furious, Tony let Richard know what he thought about this plan. But, Tony knew nothing could be done now. "The hotel utilities will be shut off soon, so we'll lose phone contact," Richard continued, ignoring Tony's outburst. "When the military comes to escort you from the hotel, they'll knock on the door and call you by name. If you don't hear your name, DO NOT open the door, or respond to any other knocks, for any reason." Tony, Paul, and Umesh resigned themselves to more delays.

~ ~ ~

Regina, Nina, Katrin, and Heidi left their suburban hotel for the airport at the same time we were leaving our hotel. Nina quickly finished one last cigarette before boarding their bus. Regina, having been able to recharge her phone, sent Lutz a text telling him they were finally leaving Mumbai. Mumbai's always crowded and chaotic traffic during the 20-minute bus ride continued to amaze Regina. Beggars waved to the bus whenever it stopped, and Regina watched the goats in the street. At the airport, the GIA inbound crew, like our Flight 36 crew, left to do their pre-flight checks while Regina and the other attack survivors walked towards the GIA ticket counter to pick up their tickets for the flight home to Frankfurt. As she turned towards the counter, Regina saw something out of the corner of her eye: US! She quickened her step, hurried toward us, her heart racing, overjoyed to see us alive and safe.

~ ~ ~

An avid reader, I was never without a book. In my crew bag, still in the wreckage of the Trident-Oberoi, was the book I was currently half-way through, a biography of Madeline Albright. As I stood near the TIA ticket counter, I realized I had nothing to read on the long flight home. My wallet held about 400 rupees, not enough to buy a book but hopefully a magazine of some sort, and I turned to look at a news stand. With my back to the group, I didn't see Regina approach. Mary did, and from behind me I heard Mary cry "OH!!! OH!!! OH!!!"

Mary wrapped her arms around Regina, overjoyed beyond words to see her. I spun around to see why Mary was crying out, and when I did, I rushed over, all thoughts of a magazine forgotten. Locked in a life-or-death embrace, Regina asked Mary, "Are you alright?" "YES!" cried Mary, in the first emotional release I'd seen from her. As soon as Mary let go of Regina, Paula took her place, and I waited impatiently for my turn! The moment I could, I enveloped Regina in a bear hug, emotionally overwhelmed to see her, so overwhelmed I couldn't immediately speak. I was beyond grateful to Regina for being able to contact her husband and thus GIA; I felt she was truly responsible for saving our lives. Our TIA crew couldn't contact anyone, but Regina could and did. I was so overcome and so utterly speechless that I couldn't find the words to express my gratitude. ("Speechless" isn't a word that's usually associated with me!) When I finally felt I could speak without breaking down in tears, I stood back from Regina to look her directly in the eyes. Holding both of her hands in mine, I said, "I'm so glad you're safe. You're safe." So many thoughts scrambled in my brain, and I felt like a fool, unable to express myself. When I finally let go of Regina's hands, I saw Katrin and Nina and the rest of the GIA crew with whom we'd shared the barricaded conference room. Nina let go of Katrin long enough to allow me to hug them both. The first of many tears I would shed over the events of the past days began to flow, and I wasn't the only one crying. Reluctantly, I waved goodbye to everyone as they headed to the GIA ticket counter. I later kicked myself for not exchanging contact information with the GIA crew members with whom I had shared this traumatic experience.

~ ~ ~

At the TIA ticket counter, Sam and Captain Marvin collected our tickets from the agent. The tickets were merely a formality to make it easier to go through the security checkpoint, customs, and immigration. Debra, Anne, and the rest of the inbound Flight 36 crew would work the flight while my crew and I would fly as passengers. Technically, the flight was cancelled and was operating simply as a ferry flight without paying passengers. Although local traffic had been rebooked to the extent possible, there were some 15 or 16 passengers leftover who were transiting through Mumbai. The ticket agent asked Captain Marvin if he'd mind carrying them. Captain Marvin agreed, and those passengers were accommodated in the main cabin while my crew and I were seated in business class.

~ ~ ~

Back in Chicago, Joee located contact information for the American consulate in Mumbai and called it. He thought that, if I had truly lost everything, I might seek help from the consulate. Unable to provide specific information about me, the consulate simply told Joee that all the Americans were being protected and that anyone who wanted to leave was doing so. Rattled, Joee called everyone he could think of to alert them to my plight and to seek support in what he experienced as a difficult time. Joee's partner, Scott, reluctantly agreed to attend his family's Thanksgiving celebration without Joee because Joee wanted to be able to monitor his e-mail and quickly respond if I needed him. Among those providing support to Joee were the other two Leatherman I considered brothers, Don and Rob, along with Dean Ogren, a community leader and mentor to us all. As well as being friends, Dean, Joee, Joanne, and I were all neighbors, living within a few blocks of each other.

Don and his partner Brad were in Florida for the long holiday weekend. Rob was working at the front desk of a large downtown Chicago hotel. And Dean was at his parents' home in Wisconsin. Hearing Joee's distress and considering my situation, Dean calmly and rationally asked, "Do I need to come home now?" "No," Joee responded, "there's nothing you can do here. I'll let you know as soon as Doug's home." Dean said he was due to return home to Chicago on Friday, and he told Joee to bring me over whenever I got home because he'd be bringing home plenty of food from his parents' Thanksgiving dinner. Rob, too, remained calm, telling Joee to keep him apprised of the situation. Rob sent me a text, hoping I'd be able to see it. Don was enjoying a beer by a pool when Joee reached him on his cell phone. Absorbing the news and realizing Joee was shaken, he simply asked, "Do I need to come home? I can get on a plane tonight." "No," Joee responded, "I'll keep you up to date. Keep your phone handy." Don then sent me a text promising me he'd see me the moment he got home. With nothing more to do, Joee collapsed on his couch.

~ ~ ~

On Thursday, after talking with Joee and getting his assurance he'd let her know what was going on, Joanne reluctantly left for Thanksgiving with her friends and her wedding officiant obligations. Desperate for any word about me, Joanne continually checked her e-mail and stared at her silent cell phone. Telling her friends about my plight, Joanne stressed that our last words before I left were "I love you." "That's a lesson I'll never forget," Joanne said. Joanne and her friends said a prayer for my safety.

~ ~ ~

On the phone with our parents, my brother Andy explained what he knew. "The hotel was bombed and set on fire. Doug escaped under actual gunfire. He lost everything, including his cell phone. But he's unhurt, safe, and on his way home." My Mom thanked God I was alright, and she focused on the fact I was alive and uninjured. My Dad asked when—and how—I was getting back to Chicago. Andy didn't know, but he assured them he'd let them know the details as soon as he got them. Quietly, so as not to frighten the children, my parents told my sister and her husband what had happened. Uncertainty was their only certainty.

~ ~ ~

After passing through security in the Mumbai airport, I joined the others for the walk to the departure gate. Of all things, Nicolas and Juan stopped for Kentucky Fried Chicken on the concourse! Samantha, Debra, Anne, and the rest of the Flight 36 crew boarded first, followed by my crew, then the few passengers. I chose a seat on the right-hand side of the plane next to a window with the intention of sleeping on the long flight to Amsterdam. I was happy to have an empty seat next to me so getting up to use the restroom wouldn't disturb anyone. Colleen and Nicolas were a few rows in front of me. A few of my crew chose the center tier of seats, with David and the rest across the plane along the left-hand side windows. Anne's jump seat was at the boarding door just behind David.

In the deserted rear of the cabin, moments before the plane turned onto the runway, Samantha texted her sister that they were leaving Mumbai bound for Amsterdam.

When the aircraft roared down the runway, David could no longer hold back the tears. His stoic façade broke, and tears rolled down his cheeks. Hearing his sobs, Anne hurried to his side, took his hand, and sat with him, offering both comfort and support.

At last, we were leaving our ordeal in Mumbai behind, and we were on the first leg of our journey home.

~ ~ ~

After takeoff, with tears in her eyes Debra rose from her jump seat and stepped over to Samantha, standing at the rear galley. Without a word, the two women hugged, and Debra shook with sobs of relief.

With only 16 passengers to serve in the mid-main cabin, instead of a full load of 260, the working flight attendants had little to do. After pulling herself together, Debra walked to the business class cabin to offer assistance to that cabin's flight attendants in serving my crew and the pilots flying the plane. Sam passed paper and pen to us, instructing us to write down our name, employee number, and the destination to which we wanted to fly once we got to Detroit. I added my information and my request to be flown to Chicago's O'Hare International Airport.

I was lightly dozing when Debra woke me with my dinner. "What can I get you to drink?" she asked. "I wish I could have a beer," I sighed.

Being in uniform, I was forbidden by federal air regulations to drink alcohol. "You're not working, and to me that no longer looks like a regulation uniform! After all you've been through, you deserve all the beer you want!" Debra chuckled. She returned from the galley with two beers for me. We both laughed, then I relaxed with my dinner, the beer, and the movie *Mama Mia* on the in-seat television screen.

~ ~ ~

Exhaustion. Dehydration. Emotional trauma. We were all succumbing to their effects. Despite the beer, I couldn't sleep, and I was jealous of the sound sleep that had claimed Colleen and Nicolas. On their crew breaks, Samantha and Debra availed themselves of the plane's crew bunks to get some much-needed sleep. The crew members on duty were huddled in the front and rear galleys. The plane was dark and quiet, illuminated only by the moving map display on the screen at the front of each passenger cabin. As we flew over the Middle East and then Europe, we could see our progress during the nearly 10 hour flight. Missing my book and eventually getting bored with the movies, I got up to stretch and walk around the cabin. I went into the mid-cabin galley to help myself to another beer, hoping it would help me sleep. A front galley flight attendant saw me and hurried to my side. "Are you alright?" she asked, with genuine concern. "Yes, thanks. Just getting a beer," I answered and then returned to my seat to watch more movies as we flew on in the dark.

~ ~ ~

My friends and family, scattered across the US, all waited for word. Joanne was on pins and needles. Andy and the rest of my family waited. My Leather brothers waited. Joee dozed on his couch, sleeping fitfully, although he did take time out to post on Facebook and other sites about how he was helping me in my hour of need.

~ ~ ~

My friends Lynn and Jessica arrived in Amsterdam on Thursday morning, November 27, on the third leg of their six-day Detroit-

Amsterdam-Washington, DC-Detroit trip sequence. The moment they arrived, they were stunned by the news of the Mumbai attack and to know several of us on the crew. Lynn was particularly shaken. Planning to go to her parents' home outside Amsterdam, Lynn wondered whether she should go. When told the news, they were also told we had all survived. Since no one knew when I'd leave Mumbai or how I'd be flown home, Jessica assured Lynn she should go see her parents because it was pointless to stay in the hotel. Reluctantly, Lynn agreed to go, giving Jessica her parents' phone number and strict instructions to call her if any information became available.

Jessica went to her hotel room for a nap. Awakening at about 3:00 pm, she went downstairs, heading outside for a cigarette. In the lobby, other crew members told her a gathering was scheduled that evening in the lobby because the Mumbai crew would indeed be coming to Amsterdam on their way back to the US. Jessica wanted to be there to be the first of my friends to congratulate me on surviving the attack. After finishing her cigarette, Jessica rushed upstairs to phone Lynn about the gathering. Lynn decided she'd rather wait and speak with me later in private.

In the Amsterdam crew layover hotel on Thursday evening, as many as 75 crew members gathered in the crew lounge and lobby to hold a vigil. At the same time, they enjoyed the hotel's generous American Thanksgiving Day dinner buffet. Hotel management told the crew members that we were on our way from India, and everyone wanted to greet us upon our arrival. The group waited, ate, and had drinks while watching the frightening images from Mumbai on the big screen televisions in the lobby. They speculated that we must have been able to quickly evacuate the hotel. Jessica and another flight attendant made arrangements with the hotel management and the bar to have drinks available for us, and a huge toast was planned for the moment we walked through the door.

~ ~ ~

We arrived in Amsterdam at 3:00 am on Friday, November 28, a cold, rainy Dutch night. I had no idea what to expect or when we were due to leave Amsterdam. At the boarding door, a Netherlands International Air (NIA) manager met the 16 inbound passengers and personally escorted them to a ticket counter to rebook them onto flights departing in the morning. Meanwhile, two other NIA managers— Douwe and Robert—escorted both TIA crews to a nearby meeting room where refreshments and assistance awaited us. Most of the working crew members, including Samantha, Debra, Anne, and Captain Marvin, wanted to leave for the layover hotel, so we parted company at the meeting room. There were tearful hugs all around, then the working crew left for their bus.

In the meeting room, we were met by the director of Amsterdam's Schiphol International Airport, a priest, a minister, and a professional crisis counselor. Although I'm not religious, I appreciated their concern about our well-being. As a group, we recommended that David meet first with the counselor, since he'd seen the worst of the violence. I stood enjoying a bottle of water, and Douwe and Robert gave each of us an "emergency kit," a bag containing a one-size-fits-all sweat suit and some basic essential toiletries. The information we had provided to Sam on the plane had been radioed to Amsterdam, and Robert and Douwe had booked our flights from Detroit to our desired destinations. It felt good to have a ticket in my hand that confirmed my seat from Detroit to Chicago's O'Hare International Airport.

We were still very concerned about Tony and Captain Daniel, and Paula asked about them. "Yes!" said Douwe excitedly. "We were told they'll be out of the hotel by mid-day tomorrow." We milled about the room as crew members took the opportunity to speak with the counselor, priest, and minister. I grew anxious to leave, feeling that my standing around was rather pointless and exasperating. I grumbled a bit; overhearing me, Juan said, "Relax, Doug. We're all wrung out. There's no sense in getting irritated." Begrudgingly I realized he was right. Taking a deep breath and a second bottle of water, I turned on my cell phone. The Dutch SIM card in the phone immediately connected, and I dialed my friend Ronald's phone number. Getting his voicemail, which I expected at that hour, I left a message that I'd been in the attack, that I wouldn't be in Amsterdam that evening, that I was on my way back to the States, and that I'd contact him when I got home. I didn't think to tell him I'd be at the Airport Hotel and that he could call me there. Eventually we were taken through back halls and a service tunnel to the Airport Hotel, where we were each assigned a room for the next two hours. We were to meet in the lobby at 6:00 am.

~ ~ ~

In my room I couldn't sleep. I feared that if I were to fall asleep I might not hear an alarm in two hours. So I took a much-needed shower and used the emergency kit's toiletries to freshen up. The emergency sweat suit was ill-fitting and, despite its bedraggled appearance, I decided to stick with my uniform. I sent two e-mails, one to Joee with my flight information and one to my ex-boyfriend, Russell who had e-mailed me when he learned I might have been in the attack. I told Russell that I was OK, that I'd lost everything, and that I'd contact him once I was home. Knowing my writing to be precise and well-constructed, Russell was disconcerted to receive my blunt, matter-of-fact e-mail, complete with typos and spelling errors! Immediately after hitting "send," my computer's battery gave a last gasp and died its power cord unusable in Europe without the current converter left in my luggage back at the Trident-Oberoi Hotel in Mumbai.

~ ~ ~

Samantha, Debra, Anne, and the rest of that crew staggered into the lobby of the Amsterdam crew layover hotel at about 3:30 am. While many of the revelers had given up waiting for the Mumbai crews to arrive, there were still a few in the lobby. They greeted the bedraggled crew, cheering them with "WELCOME BACK!!!" They barraged them with questions, "What happened?" "Are you OK?" "Tell us about it!" Jessica rushed over, ready to be the first friend to welcome me, only to be disappointed that I wasn't there. A bit overwhelmed, Debra was taken aback by the small crowd. Samantha told them that her crew had only been on the periphery and had flown out the crew that had been in the attack. "Who was on that crew?" several people asked in unison. Debra turned away momentarily, Anne caught her breath, and Samantha knew they'd have to offer the group something. Captain Marvin stepped up and addressed everyone. "All the crew members are safe," he said. "Most are on their way home although two are still in the hotel in Mumbai. They are both unhurt and safe. We all appreciate your concern." Captain Marvin collected his room key and headed to his room, followed by Debra. Samantha and Anne looked at the crowd, and tears began to roll down Anne's cheeks. "They hid," Samantha told the group, "they hid for their lives." "Who was on the crew?" someone asked urgently. "I don't know what I should say," Samantha answered, her voice trailing off. When shown the crew list printed from the computer, spirited from a resourceful flight attendant in the hotel, Samantha confirmed, "Yes, Mary was there, along with David, Doug, Paula, Juan, Nicolas, Colleen, and the pilots Ian and Sam. The other two, Captain Daniel and Tony, are OK and still trapped in the hotel." Wiping her tears, Anne said, "They went through hell! They just went through hell." The group grew quiet, as they realized how easily they could have been the ones in Mumbai. Jessica fought back tears and hurried to her room.

~ ~ ~

Ladi and Fola arrived in Lagos at 6:00 am on Friday, November 28. They weren't due home until Sunday, and they hadn't called ahead to tell anyone they were returning early. Exhausted and wrung out, they made their way through the busy airport terminal toward the taxi queue. It felt odd not having any luggage and still being in their sweat clothes. They rode home in silence, holding hands and gazing through the bright sunshine at the busy city.

At home, Ladi's mother, Miriam, ushered her grandchildren out the front door to the car that would drive them to school. After planting a goodbye kiss firmly on their foreheads, Miriam waved them off with a smile. Turning her attention to the breakfast dishes, Miriam was surprised a few minutes later to hear her son's voice calling, "Mom, we're home!" Miriam rushed to the entry hall and, at first sight, she knew something was wrong. She'd never seen her son and daughter-in-law in such a state of disrepair. They looked exhausted and shaken, and their sweat clothes were both dirty and disheveled. Their only bags were the ones under their eyes! "What are you doing home now? What's wrong??" Miriam asked, hugging them both. "Oh, Mom," Ladi said with a sigh, "we were in a terrorist attack in Mumbai." Finally safe at home, Fola began to cry. Miriam's eyes opened wide with shock.

~ ~ ~

Meeting in the Airport Hotel lobby at 6:00 am, I saw David and Ian had chosen to wear their emergency sweat suits. Sam was having an in-depth discussion with the pilots scheduled to fly us back to Detroit on TIA's regularly scheduled 8:00 am Amsterdam-Detroit flight. When we were all gathered together, the pilots began quietly asking each of us if we were alright. I remained outwardly cheerful although I was morbidly exhausted. We were ushered to the bus and driven through the cold, dark morning to the airport, accompanied by Douwe and Robert. Neither of them had slept, and they continued to show us concern and consideration. In the bus Paula again asked about Tony and Captain Daniel. Douwe assured her they were both still safe and they were expected to be evacuated from the hotel later in the day.

On the flight to Detroit, my crew members were all seated in business class. Unbeknownst to us, the boarding agents at the departure gate had quietly spoken to each of the 15 business class passengers, explaining why crew members in untidy uniforms and ill-fitting sweat suits were seated among them.

DIA managers briefed the flight crew for the 8:00 am flight, explaining that my crew would be in business class. Everyone was concerned about us and wanted to ensure that we were made as comfortable as possible. Purser Michael Ehret briefed the business class flight attendants—Gloria Chambers, Zoe Chen, and Rafael Washington—asking them to take extra special care of us. The flight attendants didn't know quite what to expect. Imaginations running wild, they wondered if we were injured or dressed in rags!

After we'd boarded the flight, Michael greeted each of us at our seat, wanting only to be sure we felt safe and welcome. Just before the cabin door was due to close for departure, Douwe's phone rang. Visibly relieved, he thanked the caller. Turning to Michael, Douwe said, "Captain Daniel and Tony have just left the Trident-Oberoi. They're finally out. Please tell their crew the good news." Michael promised he would and, as soon as the door closed, he spoke to each of us in turn, except Colleen who had already dozed off. Paula cried from relief, Mary whispered "Thank God," and I silently thanked the Universe. Indeed, now we were all safe.

Knowing what had befallen us, the married couple seated in the first row of business class, William and Susan Armstrong, approached Michael and made an extraordinarily generous offer. Handing his credit card to Michael, Mr. Armstrong offered to buy a gift for each of us who had been in the attack. We were free to choose anything we'd like from the Duty Free cart's selection of spirits, accessories, perfumes, toys, and candies. Michael was overwhelmed by the gesture. I was seated on the aisle, my preferred seat, in the third row; Colleen was directly in front of me; Sam was behind me in the window. The others were scattered about the business class cabin. Shortly after takeoff, Michael quietly approached those of us still awake and extended William Armstrong's thoughtful offer. Although I didn't want any Duty Free items, I was greatly touched by the generosity of the offer and approached the Armstrongs to thank them. William Armstrong immediately shook my hand, offering words of concern. Susan Armstrong took my hand in both of hers, looked me squarely in the eye, and asked me if I was alright and if I needed anything. Brought nearly to tears by their generosity and concern, I declined anything from the Duty Free cart and thanked them profusely for their kindheartedness. Susan, a business executive, handed me her business card, instructing me to immediately contact her if they could be of any assistance and to extend her invitation to the rest of my crew. Thanking them again, I returned to my seat and tried to relax, thinking about how a crisis can bring out the best—and sometimes the worst—

in people. I focused on the best, on all the people who were concerned about us.

~ ~ ~

My friends Lynn and Jessica met in the Amsterdam airport briefing room on Friday morning November 28; Lynn had just arrived from her parents' home. All the crew could talk about was the attack. Jessica brought Lynn up to speed, explaining that she'd met the flight 36 crew when they arrived at the crew hotel. "Doug wasn't with them, though," she explained. "The crew from the attack stayed at the Airport Hotel and went out directly on the 8:00 am flight." Lynn desperately wanted to speak with me and resolved to do so the moment they arrived in Detroit. Jessica continued to tell Lynn what she'd learned about the attack from Samantha and Anne. Lynn was gripped with terror when she learned we'd had to hide, had seen unimaginable horrors, and had run for our lives. Their flight purser, Angela Thatcher, cautioned the crew not to speak about the attack within earshot of any passengers and to try to keep their personal feelings in check. Silently, Lynn prayed that their pilots could obtain information about us by radio while in flight. Since their flight to Detroit was completely full, Lynn realized work would keep them busy and, hopefully, keep their worries on hold.

~ ~ ~

Taking Fola by the hand, Miriam led her and Ladi into their home office, not wanting the household staff to overhear. Fola sobbed, tears running down her face, unable to speak. Ladi wiped his brow with Miriam's handkerchief and asked Miriam, "Have you seen the news on television or read anything in the papers?" "No, I haven't," answered Miriam. "What happened??" Fola, regaining her composure, asked, "Are the children home?" "No," responded Miriam. "I sent them to school moments before you arrived home. Why didn't you phone so I could have sent the car for you??" "Oh, Mama," cried Ladi, his voice catching in his throat. "We were in a major terrorist attack in Mumbai. We narrowly escaped. We're lucky and grateful to be alive." Miriam looked at them, horrified. She hugged them both and said, "I'll have the children immediately brought home from school." "NO!" said Fola, wiping away her tears, "I need a nap first and I have to collect myself. They can't see their mother like this." Ladi and Fola brushed their teeth, showered, put on clean clothing, and took a nap. Once they were asleep, Miriam reached for the telephone and began calling relatives. She knew this was big news.

~ ~ ~

In the Chicago suburbs, Joanne had not had any communication from Joee, and she worried. I was so mentally muddled I didn't think clearly enough to contact her myself. Checking her e-mail and voicemail once more before going to bed Thursday night, there was no word. Sighing, she fell into a fitful sleep certain Joee would keep his promise and let her know when anything happened.

~ ~ ~

I simply could not sleep on the flight back to Detroit; my body would not relax. I sat on the plane, mindlessly watching movie after movie, some of them twice since the majority didn't interest me. The crew, Rafael in particular, ensured I had adequate water as I still felt dehydrated. They offered me whatever I might want. David, Colleen, and Nicholas slept, while Mary—like me—was unable to sleep, her mind still racing.

Restless, during the middle of the flight after the meal service when the cabin wasn't busy, I stood up to pace a bit and go to the restroom. The working crew, purser Michael, and Zoe unobtrusively kept their eyes on me.

Now that I felt relatively safe and no longer needed sheer adrenaline to cope with events surrounding me, the psychological shock was settling in. Michael and Zoe watched me and noticed that I was walking in a distracted manner. After stepping out of the lavatory, I paused at the front galley. Michael asked me if I was alright. I gave him a tired half smile. "Yes, thanks. I'm exhausted now that it's all over." "I'll bet," replied Michael. Zoe nodded in agreement. "You went through a very terrifying experience." "Yeah. We had to hide," I said, not thinking that telling Michael what happened could be traumatizing to him. "The hotel was bombed, and a group of us from my crew, along with people from GIA and Nigeria, tried to escape. We couldn't get out of the hotel, so we broke into a conference room, barricaded ourselves in, and hid flat on the floor. We had to be silent for fear of the terrorists finding and killing us. Then the Indian military came to take us out, and we had to run through the devastated lobby, through the blood and bodies of those who had been killed in the first wave." "OH!" gasped Zoe, turning away and placing her hand over her mouth. Michael nodded compassionately with fear in his eyes. Seeing their reactions, I quickly wrapped up my story. "The military got us out, and we spent the night in a nearby garage." "I'm glad you're doing OK," said Michael, composing himself. "Do you need anything? What can I get you?" "Just a bottle of water, please," I responded. Wordlessly, Zoe smiled at me and handed me the bottle of water. Thanking them both, I returned to my seat.

Michael exhaled, absorbing what I'd said, and gulped some water. Zoe grabbed a cocktail napkin and wiped her eyes. When Michael patted her shoulder, Zoe stood up, excused herself, and stepped into the nearby lavatory. Sobbing, she grabbed a handful of tissues, holding them to her mouth and nose. She hadn't been prepared to hear what I'd said, and the distant look in my eyes as I recounted the bare bones of my experience had unnerved her. Thankful for her waterproof mascara, she let the tears flow, grateful she had not been in the attack, and grateful that we had escaped physically unscathed. Collecting herself, she returned to the cabin, ready to face her passengers with confidence.

~ ~ ~

In Lagos, Ladi was up half an hour before Fola, who woke up when she heard activity downstairs that meant the children had returned home from school. She hurried downstairs to join her family. Miriam sat down with the grandchildren, wanting to speak with them before they saw their parents. "Your mom and dad are home early," she said enthusiastically. The children were delighted! "But something happened in Mumbai," she said. "They can't wait to see you and to tell all of us what happened. But before anyone says anything else, I want you to tell them how much you love them and how happy you are to have them home." Ladi entered the room and embraced his children, struggling to hold back tears. Fola followed him, hugging the children tightly and letting her tears flow. That triggered Ladi's tears, too. Puzzled by their parents' tears, the children nonetheless returned the hugs, mercifully unaware of the events in faraway Mumbai.

~ ~ ~

Regina, Katrin, Nina, and the rest of the exhausted GIA crew arrived in Frankfurt early on Friday morning. As soon as she cleared customs and immigration, Regina saw Lutz racing toward her. Embracing him like never before, safe in his loving arms, Regina finally succumbed to tears. Nina collapsed into the arms of her fiancé Joachim, and Katrin hugged her mother, Bridgette. Safe at home, all let the tears of relief flow unhindered.

~ ~ ~

Shortly before we landed in Detroit on Friday, November 28, Sam instructed each of us to deplane together because we were to be escorted as a group through customs and immigration. When we reached the arrival gate, two TIA managers boarded the plane, along with the TIA's chief pilot. Returning to the group after another trip to the restroom, I was warmly greeted by a manager. Looking over at Sam and Ian, standing with the chief pilot, I was amazed to see the ever stoic, in charge Sam shed more tears as he accepted a hug from the chief pilot. *Wow!* I thought!

My crew was escorted through customs and immigration by management, and we were met in the domestic terminal by flight attendant managers Inez Rodriguez and Charles Lee. I personally knew both Inez and Charles, and it was good to see familiar faces. Joining us was a peer-support critical incident intervention specialist, Victor

Grubbs, whom I knew from my New York City days. Victor had been specially flown in from New York to offer us whatever immediate support he could prior to the arrival of professional counselors. Inez and Charles called each of us by name and hugged us. Colleen was the first to be hugged by Inez, and it was good to see Colleen relaxing into the embrace. The whole group then headed for the airport tram that would take us to TIA's inflight offices.

Once we reached the TIA office, the chief pilot prepared to take Sam and Ian to personally debrief them before they were debriefed by a representative of the pilots' union and then flown to their respective homes. We had all been through so much together that it was difficult to part company; we bade them goodbye with more hugs.

We were treated like royalty at the TIA office, with doors opened for us and more flight attendant managers surrounding us as we approached the conference room. I barely recall walking through offices abuzz with the business of running an airline. Crew members and other airline employees glanced at our entourage, probably unaware of who we were or what was going on. Mary and David wanted to return home immediately rather than stay with our group, and their wishes were respected. Base manager Nancy Sullivan quickly made their arrangements, issuing each a positive space business class pass and appointing a manager to escort them to their departure gates. I was a little sad they didn't stay with the rest of us.

Awaiting us in the conference room were sandwiches and soft drinks, and we were encouraged to help ourselves to the refreshments. A professional crisis counselor, Rosalind Dandridge, greeted each of us as we sat at the conference table, as did both base manager Nancy and the president of the flight attendants' union, Florence Ellis. As we settled in, Nancy spoke to the assembled group and said, "Everyone, there are many more of us than there of them! I need all non-essential personnel to clear the room." Across from me at the table were Victor, Florence, and Juan. Colleen sat to my right and Nicolas to my left. The mood in the room was solemn and businesslike. Rosalind surveyed us each in turn, understanding immediately the severity of our experience.

~ ~ ~

On Friday evening in Lagos, Ladi and Fola decided that they would host a special Thanksgiving dinner at their home the following day, so they invited all of their relatives and friends. Early Saturday morning Miriam and her sister shopped for the feast. Not wishing to relive the experience multiple times, Ladi and Fola promised to tell the whole story once when everyone was together. Miriam, Fola, and others cooked while relatives and friends came together. Once everyone was seated at the table, Ladi and Fola close to their children, Ladi led the group in prayer.

"We were preparing for bed," began Ladi slowly. "We heard a massive explosion and knew something was wrong." "We quickly pulled on sweats over our pajamas, and I went to the door," continued Fola. "There was an American in the hall in front of the elevators. He was an airline steward in uniform. His eyes were big as saucers! He insisted we try to leave the hotel." Everyone listened intently, some with tears spilling over. In the silence following the conclusion of the tale, Miriam excused herself, stepped away toward the kitchen, and fainted in the hallway.

~ ~ ~

Holding Regina close, the normally stoic Lutz was moved to tears as she told him about her ordeal. Regina collapsed into bed early on Friday, too exhausted to be productive. Nina, still not herself, went to bed, clutching Joachim for dear life. Throughout that night, as she would for many nights to come, Nina relived the attack in her nightmares. Safely at home, Katrin cried tears of relief, grateful to be home and to see her loved ones. Exhausted, she looked out at the cold German landscape, thanking her good fortune. Heidi, the sole Alpine flight attendant in the GIA group, was met in Frankfurt by a GIA manager who handed her a ticket for the flight home to Geneva, courtesy of GIA. The rest of Heidi's crew remained barricaded in the

Trident-Oberoi; they were liberated on Friday along with Captain Daniel and Tony.

~ ~ ~

Friday afternoon, the Indian Special Forces soldiers finally evacuated the remainder of the Trident-Oberoi's guests and assembled them on the mezzanine level—actually outside the room in which my group had sought refuge. Tony, who had been hiding with Paul Bjornmark and Umesh Parwari in Paul's room, was tired, dehydrated, and hungry. When Captain Daniel saw Tony arrive, he rushed up to him, enveloped him in a bear hug, and told him, "As soon as we're out of here, I'll take you to lunch in the airport. We'll have whatever we want!" The group was ushered out of the hotel, passing through the devastated lobby, with some guests crying softly at the sight. Although the bodies had been removed and the blood pools covered, the wreckage was unmistakable. Tony kept his head down, trying his best not to see the ruins of the once-glorious lobby. Captain Daniel quickly put an arm around Tony, guiding him out of the building. Eager to feel the warm sunshine outside, everyone hurried out of the building and onto the busses waiting to take them to the airport.

~ ~ ~

GIA pulled out all the stops in taking care of its own crew members, as well as crew members from other airlines, stranded in the hotel after the attack. The airline assembled a crew of flight attendants and pilots to ferry an empty plane from Frankfurt to Mumbai. Each crew member aboard the special flight had been trained by the company's disaster response team to address the needs of the survivors. Joining the crew were two GIA managers, two nurses, a physician, and four crisis counselors. When the evacuees arrived at the Mumbai airport, they were escorted to the GIA ticket counter, where they were met by the doctor, nurses, managers, and counselors. Manager Holger Meyer addressed the group, greeting them first in German then switching to English, knowing it was the common language among the French, Alpine, and American air crew members in the group. "GIA is here to take you ALL home," he told them. "We have spoken to French International, Alpine International, and TIA and told them we will fly all of you to Frankfurt. From there, we'll fly you to your destinations in Geneva, Paris, and the US. We have plenty of food on the plane for you, as well as soft drinks and water. Come on, it's time to begin your journey home." There were many tears visible in the group as they left the ticket counter to go through departure formalities. The newspaper headlines, visible in all the airport shops, screamed the news of the terrorist attack, complete with frightening images. Captain Daniel kept his arm around Tony, guiding him past the shops.

~ ~ ~

Base manager Nancy addressed the group in the Detroit conference room. "Most of your flights home depart in about an hour. Later, we'll have a counseling service available to individually assist each of you, but before you leave, we want to offer you the opportunity to speak with a professional crisis counselor now. I'll turn things over now to Dr. Dandridge." Dr. Rosalind Dandridge stood up and introduced herself. "I'm a PhD crisis counselor, and I specialize in traumatic event response. You've all been in a very harrowing situation, and you need to know that your emotions right now—whatever they are—are a normal reaction to an abnormal situation." She paused, surveying us. For a moment no one spoke. Rosalind, her tone noticeably softening, asked, "Does anyone want to tell me what happened?" Not knowing where to begin, we looked back at her silently.

~ ~ ~

Preparing to pick me up at the airport, Joee again phoned my brother to tell him I was on the way home. Andy said he was going to get some sleep and asked that I call him whenever I got home. As Dean had suggested when Joee spoke to him, Joee planned to bring me from the airport to Dean's home for Thanksgiving leftovers. Joee again posted news of my return online. It being Chicago in November, Joee grabbed a coat for me and steeled himself for whatever shape I might be in when he saw me.

~ ~ ~

On their special GIA charter flight, the crew warmly greeted each passenger with a hug as they welcomed everyone aboard. Tony and Captain Daniel sat together toward the rear of the plane. The considerate and thoughtful flight attendants offered each person a bottle of water. The nightmare finally over, many tears were shed by the survivors. Captain Daniel gratefully drank his water, and before he could set the bottle down, another was placed in his hand. Nestling in an airline blanket and pillow, Tony closed his eyes. All were glad to be leaving Mumbai behind them.

~ ~ ~

In Detroit I looked around the table and then chose to be the first to speak to Rosalind. I calmly described the explosion, meeting Ladi and Fola, our unsuccessful escape attempt, and our decision to hide. I paused, wordlessly inviting others to contribute to the story. Paula asked for word about Tony and Captain Daniel, we were relieved to hear they were on their way home, courtesy of GIA. Juan told how he tried to flee but had to return up the stairs, where he met us in the stairwell. Colleen nodded, recalling the events and agreeing with our recitation, but she didn't speak. When we told of spending the night in the garage adjacent to the Trident-Oberoi, Nancy was aghast. "You spent the night in a garage??" she exclaimed. "Yeah," sighed Paula, and I nodded. With that, we ended the formal meeting, exhausted. Although I thought I was thinking clearly, I realized later that I wasn't.

Rosalind cautioned us to be discreet when telling others of our experiences because hearing the tales could cause others secondary trauma as they visualized what we'd been through. Both she and Nancy made it clear they were available to address our needs, and they each gave us their business card.

As the group broke up, Nancy took me aside to tell me she hadn't been able to contact my parents. I already knew that as they weren't home in Ohio. She also asked me if there was anyone at home to take care of me. I knew Joanne and Joee were nearby and would be available to me, so I told Nancy, "Yes, I do. Thanks." Still concerned, Nancy turned me over to manager Inez Rodriguez, who escorted me to the departure gate for my flight home to Chicago.

~ ~ ~

In the US, Thanksgiving weekend is a busy travel time, and most flights are full. When we arrived at the gate, Inez spoke briefly to the gate agent, escorted me to my seat in the first row of business class, and briefed the flight's working crew. In the gate area there were several flight attendants waiting, hoping to commute home to Chicago. When I was observed being escorted onto the plane, a buzz of speculation arose. "Why is HE being boarded??" "He's junior to me!" "Was he fired??" "What happened??" "That's Doug O'Keeffe," said flight attendant Alan Zimmer. The gate agent quickly quelled the uprising, explaining I'd been in the attack in Mumbai and was being sent home. "I hope he's alright," said Alan. Aboard the plane, I placed my computer bag into the overhead compartment, gratefully accepted a cup of water from the working flight attendant, and—in my grimy, disheveled uniform—sank into my seat. I was almost home.

~ ~ ~

In the quiet after we'd left the conference room, Nancy caught her breath and put her head in her hands, simply flabbergasted by what she'd heard. Those remaining—Union president Florence, peer support representative Victor, and counselor Rosalind— hugged. All were grateful that, despite the severity of the disaster, we'd all survived, with no physical injuries. "Oh my God," Nancy sighed, "we're lucky we didn't have 11 bodies to bring back."

~ ~ ~

On Saturday, November 29, GIA flew Captain Daniel and Tony to New York City where they were met by local managers who escorted them to their TIA domestic flights. Both of them were utterly exhausted, but they managed to express their gratitude to the managers.

~ ~ ~

When I arrived at O'Hare Airport, I expected Joee would be waiting for me outside in his car near the TIA ticket counter—although I have no idea where I got that idea! Obviously, I was not thinking clearly. I waited outside for a few minutes and then thought I should call him to see if he was on his way. After much searching, I finally found one of the rare remaining pay phones...but I didn't have any change! Exasperated, I thought, *Forget it! I'll just take the el train* (part of Chicago's elevated and subway public transit system). As I walked through the ticket lobby toward the exit, Joee, who was coming down the escalator, saw me. Walking up to me, he said, "Hey, there! Where are you going?" I merely said, "Hi. Thanks for coming to pick me up." Taking in my disheveled uniform splattered with blood and my distracted demeanor, Joee could instantly tell I wasn't myself. "Here's a coat for you. Let's go home," he said, taking charge. In the car I explained I needed to call Andy and to shop for some replacement items. "We'll call Andy the moment we get to my house, and then we can go to Target," he answered. "Dean's expecting us for dinner when we're done." I stared out the window at Chicago, thinking that I really only wanted to go to sleep in my own bed in my own home.

We arrived at Joee's house, and he immediately dialed Andy's number, waking him up. When I finally spoke to my kid brother, I cried in both relief and exhaustion. I blurted out the headlines of the story while Andy shook off his grogginess and tried to focus. Pulling myself together after the phone call, I walked the short distance to my condo to change out of my bedraggled uniform, wondering idly if the uniform would ever look clean, neat, and professional again.

Later at Dean's house just down the block, I was treated to beer and Thanksgiving foods. I told my story to Dean and Joee. They listened in silence and later broke down in tears after I left. Finally at home, I took a Tylenol PM® and slept for 13 hours.

The following day, Saturday, I replaced my phone's SIM card. My parents called that afternoon after they returned home from my sister's house. After hearing the story, my mom actually joked that I was going to give her a heart attack! My friend Orlando, with whom I had had dinner in Detroit the night before I left for Amsterdam and Mumbai, called me right after I hung up with my parents. He told me in no uncertain terms that I both needed and deserved some time off. He also stressed I was traumatized and made me promise not to agree to anything with the airline at the moment. Orlando's concern was practical, and I agreed, knowing it would take a while for me to think everything through clearly.

Joanne was due home from her weekend activities on Sunday. In my mental fog, I was pretty much only doing what was right in front of me, so I didn't think to call her. I didn't know that Joee had failed to let her know I was home and that she was still beside herself with worry. Late Saturday night, Joanne had a voicemail from Dean that merely said, "Hey! Why didn't you tell me what was going on??!" It was too late to return Dean's call, so Joanne called him Sunday afternoon before leaving her friends to return home. Hearing from Dean that I had been home since Friday, Joanne was furious with Joee. She didn't blame me at all, knowing I was probably "out of it." She and Joee eventually had words over the issue.

After speaking with Dean, Joanne immediately called me, and we cried together. Sunday evening we met for dinner. Once again, I told my story, and we shared more tears and hugs. Our earlier quarrel, which we had put aside with mutual "I love you" words as I was leaving for Amsterdam and Mumbai, was settled. We cemented our relationship as chosen family that night.

~ ~ ~

During the following week, each member of our crew was individually debriefed by TIA and the FBI. It seemed like I fielded hundreds of calls from various airline managers, union representatives, friends, and fellow flight attendants. The calls quickly became overwhelming, so I began letting them go to voicemail, returning them when I was ready. I really needed to get out of the house after the debriefings, so on the following Wednesday Joanne and I went to see the film *Milk*, about gay San Francisco superintendent Harvey Milk. Joanne recognized faces and names from her days doing AIDS-related volunteer work.

~ ~ ~

Several days after the attack, the crew luggage was recovered from the Trident-Oberoi. TIA sent inflight manager Inez Rodriguez, who'd met us when we arrived in Detroit after the attack, to Mumbai to supervise the return of our luggage from the hotel back to the US. Shaken by the devastation she saw as she worked with the hotel management, Inez only wanted to complete the job so she could return home. The Trident-Oberoi trucked the luggage to the Mumbai airport's FedEx® facility. Inez arranged to have the luggage sent to Detroit and, from there, TIA sent the luggage to our homes. Upon the luggage's arrival in Detroit, I was called and, frankly, I was stunned when I was told the luggage appeared in good condition. On December 8 FedEx delivered my luggage. Both my roller-board suitcase and my tote bag were completely wrapped in shrink-wrap plastic. I stared at the luggage sitting on my living room floor, remembering when I'd last seen it. Taking a deep breath, I cut off the plastic and opened my luggage. To my utter amazement, everything was completely intact, in perfect condition—down to an apple in my tote bag!

~ ~ ~

TIA resumed flight service to Mumbai on December 1; the crews were accommodated at the Airport Hotel until TIA could secure another hotel. Initially, crew members were understandably reluctant to work these flights. TIA first had to offer flight positions to anyone willing to work the flights or had to assign predominantly junior crew members who were sitting on-call, standing by to cover open crew positions vacated by sick flight attendants, flight attendants who'd dropped one flight for another, or for flight attendants afraid to fly into a potentially frightening situation. After the first few days of service resumption, regularly scheduled flight attendants largely resumed flying the Mumbai flights.

The Trident-Oberoi Hotel reopened for limited accommodations on December 21, 2008, although the building was still undergoing extensive repairs, with whole sections remaining closed. Over Christmas 2008 my flight attendant friends Lynn and Jessica found themselves assigned to the Mumbai trip sequence since over a major holiday it was available to them. Flying over the holiday also afforded Lynn another opportunity to spend holiday layover time with her parents in Amsterdam.

On the way to the Airport Hotel in Mumbai late in the evening on December 24, Lynn told Jessica she wanted to go to the Trident-Oberoi so she could see what I had experienced. Jessica decided to join her, and the women made plans for the following morning. On Christmas morning, they took a taxi to the Trident-Oberoi and were taken aback at the condition of the hotel. Upon entering, they were warmly greeted by a hotel host who intuitively recognized them as airline crew and thanked them for returning. Lynn explained that they were fellow TIA crew members, and they wanted to see the room in which our group had hidden during the attack. The host stepped away for a moment, returning with Mr. Singh, the assistant manager. In his small office, Mr. Singh said, "Please excuse me, ladies. May I please see your airline identification? I hope you understand that we don't want to share this information with everyone." Glad to oblige, they produced their IDs. Mr. Singh showed them to the conference room. Lynn entered, but Jessica held back, suddenly unsure if she wanted to visualize us hiding in the room. In the warm sunshine the room looked safe and welcoming. Lynn felt peaceful, knowing that the room had probably saved our lives. She and Jessica hugged, tears in their eyes. After a few minutes, they departed, thanking Mr. Singh for his courtesy. Outside, despite the heat, they both shivered.

~ ~ ~

Several days after they were safely home in Lagos, Ladi and Fola went back to their normal workday world. A week later, they returned home to find Miriam excitedly pointing to their luggage, which the Trident-

Oberoi had sent via FedEx. They were astounded that the luggage was recovered and were amazed to find everything in perfect condition.

Once our lives had returned to normal, I exchanged emails with Ladi and Fola. Every year on the anniversary of the attack we exchange e-mails, remembering a time we could never forget. Someday I hope we will meet again but under cheerful circumstances.

~ ~ ~

In the confusion of the attack and its aftermath, I failed to exchange contact information with Regina, Katrin, Nina, or any of the GIA crew. I truly feel that Regina's texts and call to Lutz from the conference room saved our lives. I wanted Regina to know I hadn't forgotten her or her role in our tale, and I wanted to thank her. I repeatedly requested assistance from TIA's director of corporate security in locating her through his counterpart at GIA. Weeks later having had no luck with that approach, I searched online and found the name of GIA's Chief Executive Officer and his business address in Frankfurt. I wrote him a personal letter explaining the circumstances and requesting his help. About 10 days after I mailed my letter, I was overjoyed to find a message from Regina in my e-mail inbox. After my initial e-mail to her in which I poured out my heart, thanking her for saving our lives, we continued to exchange e-mails periodically.

~ ~ ~

Months passed before I realized the full impact the attack had on me. By the summer of 2009, I noticed I was beginning to see things in a different light. For example, I ceased caring what people thought of me and my self-confidence soared. No longer would I tolerate people in my life who brought me down. I also quit sweating some of the small stuff life gave me instead choosing to focus more upon activities I enjoyed. My volunteerism in the gay Leather community blossomed as I realized I had more to offer to the community than I'd previously realized. In sum, my priorities shifted for the better. Why bother with things you don't enjoy? Life is short. Prioritize what pleasures you.

The psychological effects of my experience unexpectedly manifested. In April 2009, gunmen attacked an immigration office in New York State, killing several employees and causing others to hide for their lives. When I saw those images on the news, I shook and cried. Counseling enabled me to understand that my reaction to this type of tragedy was completely normal. I experienced similar feelings when two flight attendant friends had an emergency landing in August 2011, again during the terrible events at Sandy Hook Elementary School in December 2012, and again in 2014 when employees were taken hostage in a siege on a coffee shop in Sydney, Australia. Apparently my emotional reaction to tragic events is likely to be a permanent result, a reminder of my own time of terror in Mumbai.

I later learned that GIA flight attendant Nina Hoffman was very traumatized by the attack and within a short time began showing classic signs of PTSD. She suffered from debilitating panic attacks and was terrified to enter high-rise hotels. She was off work for almost a year, regularly seeing a professional critical incident counselor. She feared that her career as a flight attendant was over, since during virtually all layovers, crew members stay in high-rise hotels.

Trying to help Nina, Katrin made a reservation for them to stay overnight together at a high-rise hotel in Frankfurt. She hoped to show Nina that there was nothing to fear. Although very uncomfortable, Nina made it through the night, but she still didn't want to go into a high-rise hotel on her own.

Following that night, Nina's counselor took a different approach. She instructed Nina to wear a rubber band around her wrist; whenever Nina felt a panic attack coming on, she had to snap it HARD against her skin. Doing so, the counselor explained, would interrupt the onset of the panic attack and curb its impact. "It sort of wakes me up," Nina explained to friends. Over time the treatment worked, and Nina felt well enough to return to work. Although Nina is now able to stay at high-rise hotels, a residual effect of her experience still lingers.

~ ~ ~

I never bid to return to Mumbai, but in June 2012 TIA's scheduling computer assigned me to the Detroit-Amsterdam-Mumbai round-trip sequence in July. Understandably, I was concerned about returning to the scene, and I asked my counselor for his opinion. He whole-heartedly encouraged me to do so, as did other survivors and friends. In preparation, I e-mailed Sanjay Sheshadray, the general manager of the Trident-Oberoi Hotel, telling him when I'd be in Mumbai and asking if I could see the conference room in which our group had hidden. Very accommodating, Mr. Sheshadray immediately agreed, asking only that I phone him when I was on my way so he could schedule time to escort me.

When the crew was briefed in Detroit before the trip sequence, I took the purser Virginia aside and explained that this was my first Mumbai trip since I'd been in the terrorist attack. She was very considerate and told me to let her know if, once we were in Amsterdam, I felt I couldn't make the trip to Mumbai.

Following the terrorist attack, all the airlines that fly to Mumbai accommodate their crews in a hotel inside a secured compound in a suburb far from the city center.

Although slightly jittery, I worked the flight to Mumbai. During the flight, Laura Adams invited me to join her and other crewmembers for drinks in the crew room at the secure hotel. I appreciated the invitation, but I declined, saying I had plans. Curious, Laura asked what those plans were. I quietly explained, and Laura immediately asked, "Who's going with you?" Rather used to doing things on my own, I hadn't thought about asking anyone to accompany me. "No one," I responded. "I'll be OK alone." Sensibly, Laura said firmly, "NO WAY! I'm going with you. You should NOT go alone. Please let me do this with you." Deep down I knew she was right, so I agreed.

On July 26, 2012, in the lobby of the crew's secure hotel, I approached the concierge, Mina Sherafudin, as she worked at the concierge desk in the lobby. As I told her that I wanted to go to the Trident-Oberoi and briefly explained why, a look of shock registered on Mina's face. "I survived the attack in the Taj Mahal Hotel," Mina exclaimed. "Wanting a fresh start after that, I moved to this hotel." It was my turn to be stunned, and I immediately hurried to the end of the desk where we met in an embrace, both of us with tears in our eyes. Other employees in the lobby were surprised at the exchange and speculated as to what we must be discussing. "Yes," said Mina. "You must go back." Wiping away a tear, Mina returned to her computer. No more words were needed; we each knew where the other's thoughts had gone. In short order, Mina phoned Mr. Sheshadray, arranged a car for me, and, giving me her business card, asked me to tell her about my visit when I returned.

Laura met me in the lobby, and cameras in hand we headed downtown to the Trident-Oberoi. Laura had stayed at the secured hotel compound during previous Mumbai layovers; this, however, was the first time she had left the compound to venture into Mumbai's city center. The traffic was horrific, in part because Mumbai streets have little in the way of traffic lights or stop signs. Motorcycles darted and swerved around chaotic car and truck traffic; goats, cows, and pedestrians wandered about; beggars approached the car whenever we stopped; and slums abutted the streets, sometimes even occupying the median of a street. Laura was in awe, snapping photos the whole way.

The entrance to the Trident-Oberoi was not as I remembered it. Once open to the street, the portico was now barred by a huge gate that had to be moved whenever traffic wished to enter or exit the space. Entering the lobby required passage through a security checkpoint, the kind you'd see at an airport. I was immediately struck by the many changes that had been made to the lobby: the fountain was gone; the floor marble was a different color; and the furnishings were all new. I focused on threading my way to the front desk through the buzz of guests milling about the lobby.

At the desk I introduced myself to the clerk and told her that Mr. Sheshadray was expecting me. The clerk was a bit surprised, since a Westerner meeting with the general manager was not a routine occurrence. After phoning Mr. Sheshadray, the clerk invited us to take a seat in the lobby to await his arrival. I was somewhat nervous, both at being in the Trident-Oberoi again and wondering what to expect from Mr. Sheshadray. As he approached us, Laura and I stood to greet him. He offered the standard "Namaste" greeting, and I awkwardly shook hands with him. We chatted while he led us to the mezzanine level.

~ ~ ~

Standing at the door to the conference room in which our group had hidden, I caught my breath, seeing everything as it had been on that day. I turned to Mr. Sheshadray and asked if we might have a few minutes in the room. "Certainly," he agreed, "I'll be down the hall." Laura watched me closely as we entered the room, concern and compassion in her expression. I slowly began telling her what had happened in the room. I talked about Ladi, Fola, Regina, Katrin, Nina, Paula, Mary, Nicolas, Juan, and Colleen and pointed out where we'd each been. Lying on the floor, I told Laura how I'd seen the door from under the conference table. As I continued to recount the events, I broke down...tears rolling down my cheeks, my voice breaking. Laura embraced me in a big hug. "Oh, honey! I can't believe you're facing this after what happened." Composing myself, I replied with conviction, "I had to face this, for resolution." I asked Laura to take a few photos of me in the room so I could show my family and friends what the room looked like. I sat at the table, now elegantly set for an event while Laura took a photo. I imagined all of us gathered together in that room, although I know some of them would not have chosen to return to the scene. Our lives were saved because of that conference room and Regina's call to Lutz and GIA. Memories.

After spending about 15 minutes in the conference room, we returned to the hallway and Mr. Sheshadray. I thanked him profusely for his kindness, but he brushed that away, assuring me that he had been pleased to show me the room. I told him about the attack and how we'd arrived at the conference room after we'd tried to exit the building through a door leading outside to the pool. He quickly pointed out that door in an alcove down the hall. He told me about the attack from his point of view. He clarified some of the logistics for me, particularly the reason we'd been evacuated from the building through the devastated lobby. That route was the quickest way out from the conference room. Mr. Sheshadray told us he'd lost employees in the attack, and the survivors were, of course, greatly affected by the experience. "I understand there's a monument here," I told him. "May we see it?" "Of course," responded Mr. Sheshadray. He escorted us to the pool area outside the conference room. The monument read:

IN MEMORY OF

OUR GUESTS

AND

OUR STAFF

26th NOVEMBER, 2008

The Oberoi

TRIDENT

After seeing the monument, I was ready to leave. Not only was I emotionally drained, but I knew the return through more chaotic traffic would be stressful. Mr. Sheshadray graciously offered us lunch or tea, but I declined, explaining our time limitations. I later learned that it was the custom to accept such an offer in India, with refusal being somewhat rude. I can only hope Mr. Sheshadray understood our reason for declining. We had spent about 90 minutes at the Trident-Oberoi.

Upon returning to our hotel, I immediately e-mailed Ladi and Fola, telling them about my visit and offering to send them the photos we had taken. They gratefully accepted. Interestingly, they both remembered the room bigger than it actually was!

~ ~ ~

Flight attendant Paula Burns retired on December 1, 2013. In March 2014 Paula relocated to Santa Fe, New Mexico and became active in the local arts community. As Paula now lives relatively close to her son in Denver, she enjoys quality time with her grandchildren. Paula never returned to Mumbai.

Still based in Detroit, flight attendant Mary McAlister regularly flies to Sao Paulo, Brazil. As of this writing Mary intends to retire by 2016. Mary has never, nor will she ever, return to Mumbai.

Flight attendant Colleen Ballard is still based in Detroit and regularly flies to Tokyo or Seoul. Her daughter Lisa joined her mother on her mother's first trip sequence back to work in February 2009. Colleen will not return to Mumbai.

Flight attendant Tony Park transferred to TIA's crew base in Seattle in 2012; it's an easier commute from his home in Portland, Oregon. Tony remains in contact with both Paul and Umesh. In January 2010 Umesh invited Tony and Paul to visit him at his home in Delhi. Around seeing the Taj Mahal and other cultural sights, the three men enjoyed an emotional reunion. Tony has never returned to Mumbai.

Still a purser, flight attendant Nicholas Dumont resumed flying to Mumbai about three months after the attack and continues to do so. Nicolas and I have twice flown together to Mumbai since 2012. "Lightning can't strike twice!" Nicolas quipped upon our first time back flying together.

Flight attendant David Johnson is still based in Detroit; he prefers to fly domestic routes, often bidding to layover on the West coast. The psychological impact of the attack manifested for him several months later when he began exhibiting classic symptoms of Post-Traumatic Stress Disorder. David began experiencing insomnia and suffered terrible nightmares. At his wife Shannon's insistence David sought counseling and eventually recovered from the trauma. David will not return to Mumbai.

Flight attendant Juan Lopez transferred to TIA's New York City crew base at the end of 2009. Upon his return to work at the Detroit base, everyone with whom he flew wanted to hear about the attack; over time this became emotionally exhausting to repeat. The New York City base afforded him a much needed fresh start. Juan regularly flies to London or Dublin. He has never returned to Mumbai.

Captain Daniel individually contacted each crew member in December 2008 to check up on us; he wanted to personally hear from each of us that we were safe and well. He resumed his flight duties in February 2009 by flying back to Mumbai and continued to do so for the remainder of his career. Captain Daniel retired in January 2014 concluding 38 years as a pilot.

First officer Sam Wilson was terribly shaken by the attack and had unexplainable anger towards the terrorists who'd caused it. Realizing he needed professional help, Sam sought counseling through the VA hospital system. Sam returned to flying to Mumbai in March 2009 but prefers to regularly fly to Paris or Frankfurt. In 2011 Sam and I flew together to Paris three times in one month! We enjoyed seeing each other again.

Second officer Ian Reid returned to work in January 2009. Over the next three years Ian occasionally worked Mumbai flights but never felt truly comfortable being there. In 2012 he successfully completed captain upgrade training to become a Boeing 757/767 captain. Ian now flies either domestically or to Canada.

Flight attendant Samantha King returned to Mumbai for the first time since the attack in April 2010. On the last leg of the six-day trip sequence, on the return leg from Amsterdam to Detroit, her flight developed mechanical trouble and made an unscheduled landing in Boston. Although the plane made a safe landing, Samantha and the other flight attendants were, understandably, a bit shaken up. Her next trip to Mumbai, two months later, was uneventful. Samantha continues to regularly fly to Mumbai.

Flight attendant Debra Welsh resumed her flight schedule two weeks after the attack. In retrospect she feels now she probably returned to work too soon. While she wasn't afraid to fly, Debra realized she was having trouble focusing on her job, and she couldn't sleep on her layovers making her work physically and emotionally exhausting. At Samantha's behest Debra sought counseling. Over time Debra's emotions settled but she will not return to Mumbai.

Flight attendant Anne Fitzsimmons often flies to Mumbai, but she misses the downtown layovers. Following the attack, TIA's Disaster response team debriefed Anne to learn how she responded to the immediate needs of my crew upon arrival at the Airport Hotel. Anne was honored to share her experience; she truly feels she was just in the right place at the right time when someone needed help and she could provide it.

Captain Marvin Ross was outwardly unaffected by the attack and resumed his regular flight schedule one week later. Privately, Captain Marvin has spoken of his feelings about the attack but refuses to afford the terrorists the benefit of getting the better of him. After 37 years as a pilot, Captain Marvin retired just three months after Captain Daniel.

TIA's Mumbai station manager Raj Kansupada continues in his position.

Unbeknownst to me, GIA flight attendant Regina Schumann returned to Mumbai on a layover in February 2012. She, too, visited the Trident-Oberoi and the conference room. Achieving the resolution she sought, Regina now rarely thinks about the attack. Regina and I remain in contact. Someday I hope we will meet again.

GIA flight attendant Nina Hoffmann resumed flying in October 2009. The therapist who helped her overcome her PTSD also assisted her to successfully quit smoking shortly before marrying her fiancé Joachim in May 2010. Nina prefers to fly within Europe or North Africa but will never return to Mumbai.

GIA flight attendant Katrin Sammler, Nina's guardian during (and after) the attack, was so exhausted upon her return home that she slept nearly 13 hours her first night. Katrin did not feel the need for professional help after the attack. In January 2009 she returned to flying, requesting Mumbai as her first destination. "I wanted to face that hurdle!" Katrin told her friends. Today, Katrin regularly flies to GIA's Middle East destinations.

Alpine International flight attendant Heidi Lowe, once safely home in Zurich, was off from work until January 2009. Nightmares occasionally plagued her but by 2010 those faded. Heidi continues to fly for Alpine International now mostly to North America. Toronto is her current favorite layover. She has never returned to Mumbai.

Ladi and Fola have never returned to Mumbai, nor do they intend to do so. In the days following her return home, Fola suffered nightmares causing her to lose sleep. Speaking with her parish priest helped Fola overcome the nightmares and over time they abated. Since the attack Ladi has twice declined to return to Mumbai to conduct business dealings. Fortunately management at Nigerian Oil does not push him on the issue. We remain in email contact. Someday I would like to see them again.

Shopkeepers Amil and Mr. Gupta reopened their shops in the Trident Oberoi in December once repairs were complete. Without the crew staying in the hotel, business considerably dropped, but both merchants made trips to the new hotel to accommodate the needs of the crew members.

And me? I was off the whole of December 2008. When I announced my intention to return to work on a domestic five-day sequence departing January 3, my good friend Lynn insisted upon meeting me at the airport prior to my departure. We went to lunch and Lynn point blank asked me whether I felt safe returning to work. Her concern was heartwarming. Lynn continues to fly out of Detroit and we occasionally work together.

My brother Andy Lenart and his wife Urska still live in Missouri. Both were shaken by the whole experience and couldn't wait to have me visit their home in December 2008 while I was off from work. In 2010 my parents moved to Missouri to be near Andy and Urska. Andy continues his work as a police officer. My dad still lives in Missouri, my mom died in 2013.

In Minneapolis Director of Security Richard Santini continues in his position relieved he hasn't had another similar incident to have to manage. Assistant Director Jim Snodgrass left TIA in 2011 to become the Director of Security for a major regional airline. Margaret Olsen, the Director of TIA's Disaster response team, continues in her position. She too is grateful another "Mumbai attack" hasn't occurred. Nancy Sullivan, Detroit's base manager at the time of the attack, was promoted to a higher managerial position within TIA in 2011. Candice Price, who took Captain Daniel's calls, left TIA for a position at a major retailer in 2010. Shauna McNalley, who answered Tony's initial call from India, retired in 2012.

Joanne Gaddy moved to Florida in 2012 to escape Chicago's severe winters. We stay close and try to speak nearly every day. Joee Artega continues to live in Chicago. Though Joee shared his side of this story with me for this book, he dislikes revisiting the topic of the attack. I'm still close to my Leather brothers Don and Rob; Dean Ogren continues to live down the block from me.

My Amsterdam friends - Ronald, Leo, and Arjen - each spoke with me by phone about a week after my return home. They were beyond relieved I was home safe. I continue to regularly see them in Amsterdam.

My ex Russell called me two days after my return home to check on me. His consideration was appreciated. Coincidentally, Jessica called while I was speaking to Russell and left me a voice-mail. When I returned her call, Jessica cried from relief upon hearing my voice. Knowing people cared so much was beautiful.

~ ~ ~

Surviving a traumatic incident has taught me compassion for other trauma survivors, whatever the cause. I learned that when you've been traumatized, you're not able to think clearly, even if you think you are. It's best not to make any major decisions for a few days. Take time for yourself; know that your reactions are normal. Pace yourself. Let your friends look out for your welfare. Accept thoughtfulness and generosity from others. People feel good about themselves when they help others; let family, friends, neighbors—even strangers—feel good by making your life a little easier in a stressful time. Acknowledge that you did nothing wrong to create the situation; it simply happened. Don't let the trauma overwhelm you or redefine your identity. Most important: don't hesitate to take advantage of professional help from a psychiatrist or counselor. (Writing a book about the experience can be cathartic, too!) And remember to always say "I love you" to those you cherish.

~ ~ ~

Safe travels, everyone.

About the Author

Douglas O'Keeffe is the author of <u>Jeff's Way</u>, the true story of flight attendant Jeffrey Collman who died aboard hijacked American Airlines flight 11 on September 11, 2001. A skilled interviewer, Douglas co-produces the Leather Archives and Museum's acclaimed live-on-stage interview series *Inside Leather History, A Fireside Chat*, and is a long-time community charity volunteer. Douglas lives in Chicago and is a flight attendant for a major airline. <u>Gunfire and Silence, Surviving India's 9/11</u> is his second book.

www.ingramcontent.com/pod-product-compliance
Lightning Source LLC
Chambersburg PA
CBHW070911290526
45795CB00001B/288